JN004123

関東大震災100年

──写真に刻まれた記憶──

定点観測者としての通信社

100 Years Since Great Kanto Earthquake

— Memories Captured in Photos —

A news agency as eyewitness

公益財団法人 新聞通信調査会
Japan Press Research Institute

目次 / Contents

凡例

- 写真番号は掲載順に付している。
- 日付のない写真は日付が特定できなかったものである。
- 写真提供は共同通信社(1-23, 25-99)、鎌倉市中央図書館(24)。
- 共同通信提供の写真98枚のうち撮影元が明らかになっているものは次のとおり。
  共同通信社…39
  日本電報通信社…1, 4-11, 13, 14, 17-19, 22, 23, 25-27, 29, 31, 33, 36, 40, 44, 50, 62, 66, 67, 70, 72, 73, 75, 76, 78, 80, 81, 83-85, 90, 92, 94, 98
  君波昭治…2, 89, 91, 93, 95, 97, 99

報道写真展「関東大震災100年―写真に刻まれた記憶―」開催に当たって

日本は地震国である。去る5月11日払暁、「緊急地震速報です。強い揺れに注意してください」というスマートフォンからの警報で眠りを覚まされた。震源地は千葉県南部。それより先の5月5日には石川県珠洲《すず》市で震度6強の地震があった。30数年前、韓国ソウルに3年間駐在したが、隣国でありながら、揺れた記憶は一度もなかった。「地震、雷、火事、親父」と、日本で怖いものの筆頭に地震があるのも故なしとしない。

1923（大正12）年9月1日、東京、横浜などに未曽有の被害をもたらした関東大震災が発生した。震源地は相模湾北西部、マグニチュード7.9、死者・行方不明者合わせて約10万5000人に上った。約9割が火災による焼死だった。経済被害は東日本大震災の10倍を超えるという。翌2日の大阪朝日新聞号外は「あらゆるものは倒れた、壊れた、焼けた、死んだ」と見出しを打った。東京が焦土と化した。2023年はあれから100年になる。

両国の国技館に程近い東京都慰霊堂には何度か足を運んだ。当初は震災記念堂といったが、東京大空襲の犠牲者の遺骨も安置して今の名称になった。震災で多くの死者を出した陸軍被服廠《ひふくしょう》跡につくられた横網町公園にある。公園内には関東大震災朝鮮人犠牲者追悼碑も設置されている。震災後の社会不安に紛れ、流言飛語により多くの朝鮮人が虐殺された。震災とともに、ぜひとも記憶にとどめておくべき事件である。

9月1日の「防災の日」は、1960（昭和35）年に制定された。関東大震災に由来する。「天災は忘れたころにやってくる」とは寺田寅彦《てらだとらひこ》の名言といわれるが、平成以降は忘れぬうちにやってくる感じだ。阪神大震災（1995年）、東日本大震災（2011年）、火山の噴火、毎年のように起きる豪雨と水害……。内閣府によれば、南海トラフ地震が起きる確率は今後30年の間に70～80%、首都直下地震も同じく30年以内に70%程度という。備えが重要だ。

今回、写真展のテーマに関東大震災を選んだのは、当時を振り返り、今後の対策につなげてほしいとの思いからだ。写真展はプロローグの「100年前の新橋」から、被害の大きさを示す「失われた日常」、被災後の市民を写した「暮らしの回復」、そしてエピローグは「東京今昔～100年を経て」の4部構成とした。使用した99枚の写真の中には、当時の日本電報通信社（現・電通）が撮影し、共同通信社（共同）が保有する貴重なオリジナルネガも多数含まれている。その鮮明な画像に注目していただきたい。

写真展の開催に当たっては、共同の全面的な協力を得ました。定点観測者としての通信社の役割についてもご理解いただければ幸いです。

公益財団法人 新聞通信調査会
理事長　西沢　豊

Greeting from Photo Exhibition Organizer

Japan is an earthquake-prone country. In the early hours of May 11 this year, I was awakened by the raucous sound of an earthquake alert via my cellphone. Its epicenter was in southern Chiba Prefecture. On May 5, there was an earthquake measuring an "upper 6" on the Japanese seismic intensity scale of 7 in Suzu, Ishikawa Prefecture. More than 30 years ago, I was stationed in Seoul, South Korea, for three years, but never experienced a jolt. No wonder earthquakes head the list of things Japanese people fear most, followed by thunder, fires and fathers.

On Sept. 1, 1923, the Great Kanto Earthquake occurred, causing unprecedented damage to Tokyo, Yokohama and surrounding regions. The magnitude 7.9 quake had its focus in northwestern Sagami Bay and left about 105,000 people dead or missing. About 90% of the casualties resulted from fires. Economic damage was estimated to be over 10 times that of the Great East Japan Earthquake in 2011. The Osaka Asahi Shimbun issued an extra the following day with a headline saying, "Everything and everybody collapsed, destroyed, burned and died." Tokyo was in rubble. This year marks the 100th anniversary of the Great Kanto Earthquake.

I have visited the Tokyo Metropolitan Memorial Hall near the Ryogoku Kokugikan arena a number of times. It was originally called the Earthquake Memorial Hall but changed to its present name after adding the ashes of victims of the Great Tokyo Air Raids during World War II. It is located in Yokoamicho Park which was built on the former Imperial Army Clothing Depot where many lost their lives after taking refuge to flee fires triggered by firestorms. Also standing in the park is a memorial monument to Korean victims of the Great Kanto Earthquake and its aftermath. Many Korean residents were massacred due to false claims made against them during the confusion following the quake. It is an incident people definitely should remember.

Disaster Prevention Day on Sept. 1 was so designated in 1960 to remind the Japanese people of the Great Kanto Earthquake. Natural disasters occur when people forget about them, as Japanese physicist and author Torahiko Terada famously said. Such disasters have happened fairly frequently even during the Heisei Era (1989-2019). Recent examples include the Great Hanshin Earthquake in 1995 and the Great East Japan Earthquake and tsunami in 2011, as well as volcanic eruptions and frequent floods caused by torrential rains. According to the Cabinet Office, there is a 70-80% chance of a Nankai Trough earthquake occurring and about a 70% chance of a Tokyo inland earthquake in the next 30 years. We have to be prepared.

We have chosen the Great Kanto Earthquake as the theme of our latest photo exhibition to reflect on its history and help it chart a future strategy. The exhibition consists of "Shimbashi 100 Years Ago," "Lost Daily Lives" showing the extent of damage, "Restoration of Living," and "Tokyo Past and Present over 100 Years." Among the 99 photos on display are those of many valuable original negatives shot by Nippon Dempo Tsushinsha (present-day Dentsu Group Inc.) and currently in the possession of Kyodo News. We invite you to take a close look at their clear images.

We have obtained the full cooperation of Kyodo News in holding this photo exhibition and appreciate your understanding of a news agency's role as an eyewitness.

Yutaka Nishizawa
Chairman
Japan Press Research Institute

プロローグ：100年前の新橋

Prologue: Shimbashi 100 Years Ago

新橋駅と汐留駅

1872（明治5）年10月、新橋―横浜間に日本初の鉄道が開通した当時、新橋駅は現在の汐留にあった。1909（明治42）年に電車専用で日本初の高架駅として烏森駅が新橋駅の約300メートル西に建設され開業、ここを起点に品川―新宿―池袋―田端―上野を結ぶ山手線が運行開始した。

さらに14（大正3）年、東京駅開業に合わせて烏森駅が新橋駅と改称され、それまでの新橋駅は貨物列車専用の汐留駅となった。ちなみに上野―東京間がつながり山手線が環状線として完成したのは25（大正14）年11月だ。

関東大震災が起きた時は新橋、汐留両駅が併存していたことになる。汐留駅は開業以来の駅舎が焼失し、34（昭和9）年に鉄筋コンクリート2階建てに建て替えられた。しかし、86年に貨物駅としての汐留駅も廃止された。跡地は96（平成8）年、駅舎とプラットホームなど基礎部分の遺構が国の指定史跡となり、2003年には開業当時の駅舎を再現した「旧新橋停車場」が建てられた。

一方、烏森駅から改称された2代目の新橋駅は建築家辰野金吾《たつのきんご》の設計になる万世橋《まんせいばし》駅を参考にしたルネサンス様式のれんが造りで、関東大震災で駅舎内部を焼失する被害を受けたものの外観は残ったため、改修して70（昭和45）年の撤去まで使用された。

Shimbashi Station and Shiodome Station

When Japan's first railway line opened between Shimbashi and Yokohama in October 1872, Shimbashi Station was located in the present-day Shiodome district. Karasumori Station, located about 300 meters west of Shimbashi Station, began operations as the first elevated station exclusively for passenger trains in 1909, inaugurating the Yamanote Line linking Shinagawa, Shinjuku, Ikebukuro, Tabata and Ueno.

In 1914, Karasumori Station changed its name to Shimbashi Station to coincide with the opening of Tokyo Station and the hitherto Shimbashi Station was reborn as Shiodome Station exclusively for freight trains. The Yamanote Line was completed in November 1925 as a loop line following the linkage between Ueno and Tokyo stations.

Shimbashi and Shiodome stations were operating side by side when the Great Kanto Earthquake struck. The Shiodome Station building was destroyed by fire, and a two-story reinforced concrete building was built in November 1934. Shiodome Station as a freight train station closed in 1986. The remains of its station building and platform foundations were designated as government-specified historic sites in 1996, and Old Shimbashi Station, a replica of its original station, was built in 2003.

Meanwhile, the second-generation Shimbashi Station, a Renaissance-style structure patterned after Manseibashi Station designed by architect Kingo Tatsuno, had its interior damaged by fire but its exterior survived. The station building was repaired and used until 1970.

1. 焼け落ちた新橋駅
Shimbashi Station burns down

屋根が焼け落ち外壁だけ残った2代目の新橋駅（左）。関東大震災発生の夜に火が回った＝1923（大正12）年

The ruins of second-generation Shimbashi Station (L) which burned down following the Great Kanto Earthquake.(1923)

2. 100年後の新橋駅
Shimbashi Station 100 years later

朝日を受けるJR新橋駅汐留口。高架には東海道新幹線が通る。右側には新交通システム「ゆりかもめ」新橋駅がある＝2023（令和5）年5月2日

Sunshine brightens up JR Shimbashi Station's Shiodome exit. The Tokaido Shinkansen Line runs on elevated tracks and Shimbashi Station on the new transit waterfront line Yurikamome is on the right. (May 2, 2023)

関東大震災～10府県襲った複合災害

日本の災害史上、飛び抜けて大きな人的被害となった関東大震災をもたらした地震は、「関東地震」や「大正関東地震」と呼ばれる。相模湾の海底などを延びる「相模トラフ」で発生。相模トラフでは、江戸時代に起きた1703年の元禄関東地震以来、220年ぶりの巨大地震だった。

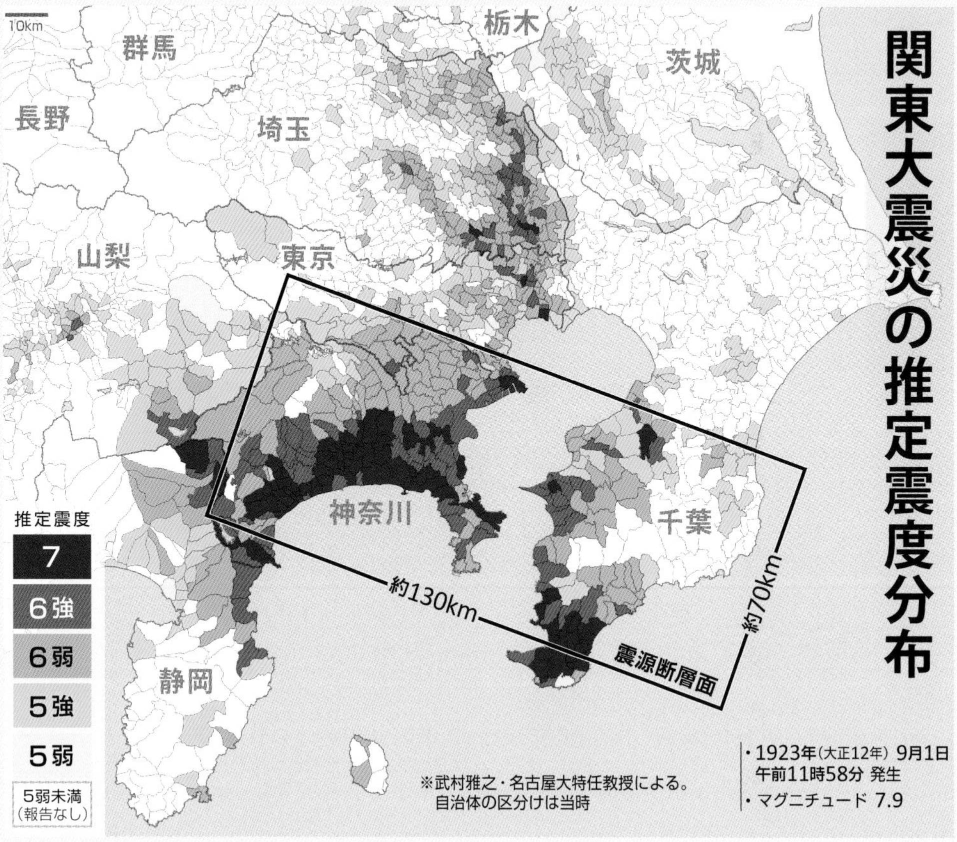

余震もM7

相模トラフでは、フィリピン海プレートと呼ばれる海側のプレート（岩盤）が、日本列島がある陸側のプレートにぶつかり、沈み込んでいる。その過程でひずみが蓄積し、限界に達すると大規模な断層破壊が生じる。この仕組みで、海溝型と呼ばれるプレート境界の巨大地震が繰り返し起きてきた。

大正関東地震は1923（大正12）年9月1日午前11時58分に起きた。マグニチュード（M）は7.9とされ、震源断層の大きさは長さ約130キロ、幅約70キロ。当時は震度7がなかったが、広範囲が震度7～6相当の揺れに見舞われた。

規模の大きな余震が多かったのも特徴だ。本震の約3分後、午後0時1分ごろの余震はM7.2、0時3分ごろの余震はM7.3と推定される。この二つを含めM7以上の余震が6回起きた。

関東大震災による住家被害と死者・行方不明者

	住家被害棟数		死因別の死者数（行方不明者含む）				
	合計	うち焼失	住家全壊	火災	流失・埋没	工場などの被害	合計
神奈川県	12万5577	3万5412	5795	2万5201	836	1006	3万2838
東京府	20万5580	17万6505	3546	6万6521	6	314	7万387
千葉県	1万9976	431	1255	59	0	32	1346
埼玉県	8845	0	315	0	0	28	343
山梨県	2802	0	20	0	0	2	22
静岡県	9259	5	150	0	171	123	444
茨城県	483	0	5	0	0	0	5
長野県	88	0	0	0	0	0	0
栃木県	4	0	0	0	0	0	0
群馬県	45	0	0	0	0	0	0
合計	37万2659棟	21万2353棟	1万1086人	9万1781人	1013人	1505人	10万5385人

※東京府は当時。武村雅之・名古屋大特任教授らによる

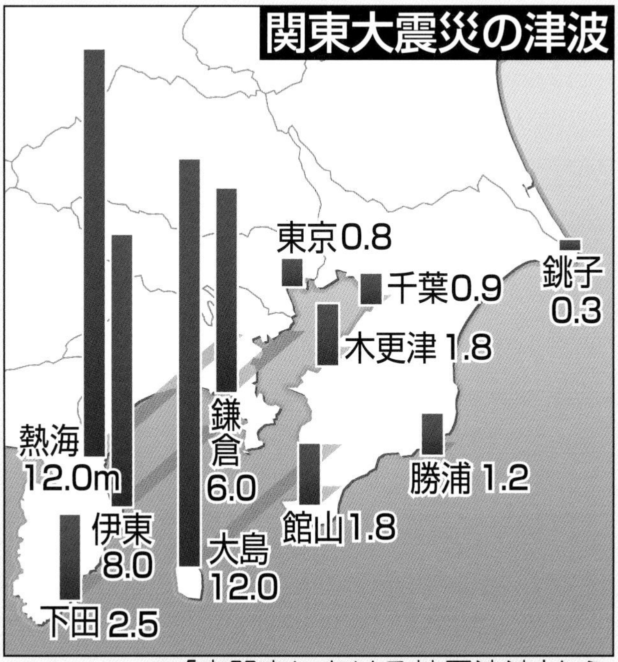

※「南関東における地震津波」から

延焼拡大

武村雅之《たけむらまさゆき》・名古屋大特任教授の調査によると、人的被害、住家被害は主に1府9県（当時は東京府）に及んだ。木造家屋や建物が倒壊、火災や津波、山崩れなどが相次いだ複合災害だった。

特に火災は、犠牲者約10万5000人のうち、約9万2000人分の死因を占める。地震の発生時間が昼食時で多くの家庭が火を使っており、気象条件も悪かった。同時多発した火災が台風の影響による強風にあおられ、消防設備が地震で損傷して使えず、密集した木造住宅で延焼が広がった。

最も悲惨な現場は、現在の東京・両国国技館に近い旧陸軍被服廠跡地だった。約6万6000平方㍍の広大な空間を格好の避難先として、多くの避難者が集まって、すし詰め状態になっていた。持ち込まれた大量の家財道具に火の粉が燃え移り、竜巻のように火災が吹き荒れる「火災旋風」が発生。この場所だけで約3万8000人が命を落とした。

倒壊、津波も

家屋倒壊による死者も約1万1000人に上る。稼働中だった多くの工場も倒壊し、工場で約1500人が犠牲になった。

箱根や丹沢など山間部を中心に土砂災害も多発した。根府《ねぶ》川《かわ》駅（現神奈川県小田原市）では、進入していた列車が地滑りで駅とともに海に転落、乗客らが亡くなった。

津波も伊豆半島東岸や相模湾沿岸、房総半島などを襲い、現在の静岡県熱海市では高さ約12㍍に達したとされる。

3. 東京駅の新聞売り
Newspaper girls at Tokyo Station

東京駅前で新聞を売る女学生。東京市内の多くの新聞社が社屋を焼失した。社屋が残ったのは3社。焼失を免れた社も停電や活字の散乱などで通常の発行がストップしたが、2社はその日のうちに号外を発行。通信網が途絶しラジオ放送が始まる前の時代、被災者に対する唯一の地震情報だった＝1923（大正12）年

Schoolgirls sell newspapers in front of Tokyo Station. Many newspaper buildings in Tokyo were destroyed by fire. Three newspaper publishers saw their buildings survive the disaster. They could not publish newspapers on schedule due to power failures and scattered typesets but two of them put out extras on the day of the quake. Newspapers were the only medium to provide earthquake information to survivors due to communications network breakdowns and the absence of radio broadcasts. (1923)

関東大震災とメディア

関東大震災により、20社近くあった東京市内の日刊新聞社はほとんどが社屋を失い、焼け残った東京日日(毎日新聞の前身)、報知(読売新聞の前身)、都《みやこ》(東京新聞の前身)3社も活字ケースの倒壊などで通常の発行ができなくなった。交通機関や電信電話回線のほとんどが不通になった。

東京日日や報知は散乱した基本活字を拾い集め、第1号外を手刷りしたり、謄写《とうしゃ》版(ガリ版)印刷したりして街頭に張り出し、避難所に配布した。朝日は東京朝日の社屋が全焼。交通、通信も途絶したため、新聞発行が不可能になって数日間休刊した。その後1カ月間は大阪朝日新聞でカバーした。

通信社は電通(日本電報通信社)と帝通(帝国通信社)も社屋を焼失。後の共同通信・時事通信に至る国際通信社も東京での業務機能がほぼ停止した。

東京—大阪の予約電話線が切れたことから事態の重大性を直感した国際通信社大阪支社が、余震が続いている最中にロンドンのロイターに第一報を打電した。その後のニュースは横浜に停泊中のシカゴ丸が発した無線を大阪の無線電信局で受信し、これを大阪支社が打電した。国際通信=ロイター電は世界的に大成功を収めた。

当時のメディアは新聞だけで、震災によって発行体制に大きな被害を受け、事実上の一時休刊を免れなかった。その間に「富士山大爆発」や「東京に大津波」などの流言が広がり人々はパニックに陥った。

各紙が発行体制を確立してからは被害の惨状を物語る写真を駆使して震災報道に全力を注いだ。大震災はその後の新聞発行部数の急速な増加を促すきっかけになった。しかし、一方で震災時の混乱から生まれたデマや根拠のないうわさを効果的に抑えられず、朝鮮人虐殺といった事態を助長する役割を果たしてしまった。

ラジオ放送は研究・試験段階だったが、大震災をきっかけに早期開局の機運が高まった。1925(大正14)年3月22日、公式ラジオ放送が開始され、同年7月12日に東京放送局(NHKラジオ第一)での本放送が始まった。

Great Kanto Earthquake and Media

The Great Kanto Earthquake destroyed the buildings of nearly 20 daily newspaper publishers in Tokyo. The Tokyo Nichi Nichi Shimbun (a precursor to the Mainichi Shimbun), the Hochi Shimbun (the Yomiuri Shimbun) and the Miyako Shimbun (the Tokyo Shimbun) survived but could not publish their papers as usual because of the collapse of their typecases and for other reasons. Transportation facilities and telegraph and telephone lines were shut down.

The Tokyo Nichi Nichi Shimbun and the Hochi Shimbun collected scattered basic movable types and printed extras manually, putting out mimeographed editions for posting on the street and distribution to shelters. The Asahi Shimbun's Tokyo building was burned to the ground and could not publish for several days due to traffic and communications breakdowns. The Osaka Asahi Shimbun covered news for its Tokyo unit for the next one month.

The offices of Dentsu (Nippon Dempo Tsushinsha) and Teitsu (Teikoku Tsushinsha) news agencies were destroyed by fire. Kokusai Tsushinsha, a precursor to Kyodo News and Jiji Press, was forced to halt its operations in Tokyo.

Alarmed by the seriousness of reserved telephone line breakdowns between Tokyo and Osaka, Kokusai Tsushinsha's Osaka branch sent out a bulletin to Reuters in London while aftereffects continued. The news agency dispatched subsequent news stories by monitoring wireless information sent out by the Chicago Maru anchored in Yokohama, making dispatches credited to Kokusai Tsushin / Reuters globally successful.

Newspapers were the only medium at the time, and the earthquake inflicted extensive damage on their publishing operations, forcing them to temporarily suspend publication. In the meantime, rumors such as a large-scale eruption of Mt. Fuji and huge tsunami hitting Tokyo sent local people into a panic.

As the newspapers reestablished their operations, they focused their efforts on their quake coverage by making heavy use of disaster photos. The earthquake helped to spur a surge in newspaper circulations. But they failed to effectively keep down rumors and groundless gossip, helping to foment tragic episodes such as the massacre of Koreans.

Radio broadcasts were in the stage of experimental and trial runs, but the earthquake heightened the movement for their early start. Public radio broadcasting began on March 22, 1925, and the Tokyo Broadcasting Station (present-day NHK Radio 1) formally started radio broadcasts on July 12.

第１章：失われた日常

Chapter 1 : Lost Daily Lives

4. 炎上する有楽町
Yurakucho on fire

地震直後に出火し燃え上がる有楽町付近を数寄屋橋方向から見る人たち。煙の向こう側は警視庁、左の鉄道ガードの奥は日比谷交差点方向＝1923（大正12）年9月1日

People in Sukiyabashi district watch Yurakucho area and its vicinity on fire. Beyond the smoke is the Metropolitan Police Department, and behind the railroad overpass on the left is Hibiya Crossing. (Sept. 1, 1923)

5. 東京電灯と帝国ホテル
Tokyo Dento and Imperial Hotel

震災後の火災で焼け落ちた有楽町の東京電灯本社(右後方)。左は開業披露当日の帝国ホテル。強い揺れに崩れることなく、従業員らの尽力により延焼を防止することができた。被害が最小限に食い止められ、外国公館や被災企業の復興の拠点として開放された=1923(大正12)年9月1日

A fire destroys the headquarters of Tokyo Dento Kabushiki Kaisha (Tokyo Electric Light Co.) (rear right). On the left is the Imperial Hotel on its opening day. The hotel survived the temblor while employees and others prevented the blaze from spreading. Damage was limited to the minimum, and the hotel operated as a reconstruction base for diplomatic missions and affected companies. (Sept. 1, 1923)

6. 猛煙に包まれた東京電灯付近
Thick smoke engulfs Tokyo Dento and vicinity

猛煙に包まれた有楽町の東京電灯本社付近。東京電灯は東京電力の前身で、日本初の電力会社。手前は帝国ホテルの工事現場＝1923（大正12）年9月1日

Thick smoke envelops Tokyo Dento and its vicinity. Tokyo Dento, a precursor to Tokyo Electric Power Co., was the first Japanese electric company. At forefront is the Imperial Hotel's construction site. (Sept. 1, 1923)

7. 炎上する帝劇、警視庁
Imperial Theater and MPD ablaze

麹町区有楽町（現在の千代田区）にあった警視庁（右）から延焼し炎上する帝国劇場（中）。左の東京会館は焼失や倒壊は免れたが大きな被害を受けた＝1923（大正12）年9月1日

A fire at Metropolitan Police Department (R) in Yurakucho, Kojimachi Ward (present-day Chiyoda Ward), spreads to the Imperial Theater (C), causing extensive damage to Tokyo Kaikan Building on left. (Sept. 1, 1923)

8. 焼け野原の京橋、銀座
Charred Kyobashi and Ginza

一面焼け野原となった京橋付近と銀座方面(右側)。被災した市電が残る大通りを人力車や馬車、自転車などが行き交う=1923(大正12)年

Kyobashi and Ginza (R) are destroyed by fire. Streetcars remain abandoned, and rickshaws, horse-drawn carriages and bicycles crisscross the streets. (1923)

9. 焼け落ちた上野駅
Ueno Station burns down

震災から数日後、上野の山から望む焼け落ちた上野駅。後方中央は浅草方面で、折れた「凌雲閣」(通称・浅草十二階)が見える＝1923(大正12)年9月

Ueno Station a few days after the earthquake and fire. In the rear center is the 12-story Asakusa Ryounkaku tower. (September 1923)

10. 日本橋の惨状
Nihombashi area in tatters

関東大震災で「日本橋」もブロンズの照明灯、欄干などが破損したが、橋そのものは石造りのため大きな被害は受けなかった。しかし、日本橋付近は地震後に発生した火災の被害が大きく、東洋一の百貨店と呼ばれていた「三越」や「白木屋」も焼け落ちた＝1923（大正12）年9月

Nihombashi Bridge's bronze lamps and balustrades are damaged in the earthquake but its stone bridge proper is not. Damage from post-quake blazes around the bridge was huge, however, and destroyed Mitsukoshi department store, touted as Asia's largest at the time, and Shirokiya department store. (September 1923)

11. 再建中の歌舞伎座と付近の焼け跡
Kabuki-za razed while under reconstruction

関東大震災後の火災で、骨組みを残して焼失した工事中の歌舞伎座。1921（大正10）年10月、漏電により全焼、再建工事中だった。工事は中断したものの、鉄筋コンクリートを使用した耐震耐火建築として1924（大正13）年暮れに完成した＝1923（大正12）年

Kabuki-za theater in ruins. It was under reconstruction when a fire razed it in the earthquake. A short circuit had burned down the theater in October 1921. The theater was rebuilt as a quake-resistant reinforced concrete structure at the end of 1924. (1923)

12. お堀端の崩落
Collapsed sloping moat earthworks

九段上停留所付近（現在の千代田区）のお堀端の崩落。地震で緩んでいた斜面が長雨で崩れた。かつての江戸城の石垣は大きな地震のたびに崩れ、修復された。関東大震災でもお堀の各所で石垣が崩れ修復工事は長期間続いた＝1923（大正12）年10月12日

The Imperial Palace's sloping moat wall near Kudan district (present-day Chiyoda Ward) collapses due to prolonged post-quake rain. Edo Castle's stone walls crumbled after frequent earthquakes and were rebuilt. Many stone walls also gave way in the Great Kanto Earthquake and repair work lasted over an extended period of time. (Oct. 12, 1923)

13. 被災した永代橋
Heavily damaged Eitaibashi Bridge

深川と日本橋を結ぶ、隅田川に架かる永代橋（左側）も大きく被災した。手前から右奥は、老朽化した永代橋を架け替えるため設置された仮橋が焼け落ちたもの。架け替えられた永代橋は1926（大正15）年12月に開通式が行われた＝1923（大正12）年9月

Heavily damaged Eitaibashi Bridge (L) over Sumida River linking Fukagawa and Nihombashi districts. From front to rear right are the remains of a temporary bridge. Newly built Eitaibashi Bridge opened in December 1926. (September 1923)

14. 焼け野原と横浜駅
Yokohama in ruins

桜木町付近から見た一面焼け野原となった横浜市の惨状。遠方の建物は2代目横浜駅（現在の横浜市営地下鉄高島町駅付近）。関東大震災で駅舎が焼失、1928（昭和3）年に現在の位置に3代目横浜駅が開業した。初代横浜駅は現在の桜木町駅にあった＝1923（大正12）年9月

The devastated city of Yokohama, as seen from near Sakuragicho. In the distance is second-generation Yokohama Station (near present-day Takashimacho Station on the Yokohama Municipal Subway). Its station building was destroyed by fire, and third-generation Yokohama Station opened in 1928, as it stands today. The original Yokohama Station was located at present-day Sakuragicho Station. (September 1923)

被災文学者の言葉
Famous Writers Chronicle Great Kanto Earthquake

関東大震災が起きた大正後期はさまざまな流派の文学者が東京にひしめき、日本の現代文学史上百花繚乱の時代だった。彼ら彼女らが残した言葉から被災の実像を垣間見る。

In the late Taisho Era (1912-1926) when the Great Kanto Earthquake occurred, many great writers of various genres lived in Tokyo, producing a simultaneous emergence of many talents and achievements. Here is a glossary of excerpts from their works (with their age at the time of the earthquake in parentheses).

柳田国男(48)　民俗学者
Kunio Yanagita (48), folklorist

(震災当時ロンドンに滞在)

所所深川あたりの狭苦しい町裏に住んで、被服廠に遁げ込んで一命を助からうとした者の大部分は、寧ろ平生から放縦な生活を為し得なかった人々では無いか、彼等が他の碌《ろく》でも無い市民に代わって、この惨酷なる制裁を受けなければならぬ理由はどこに在るか。

──『青年と学問』

永井荷風(43)　作家
Kafu Nagai (43), novelist

(東京麻布・市兵衛町、木造の西洋館「偏奇館」で被災)

日将《まさ》に午ならむとする時、大地忽《たちまち》鳴動す。(中略)門外塵烟濛濛《じんえんもうもう》、殆《ほとんど》咫《し》尺《せき》を弁ぜず。(中略)余も亦徐《またおもむろ》に逃走の準備をなす、時に大地再び震動す。書巻を手にせしまま表の戸を排《おしひら》いて庭に出づ。数分間にしてまた震動す。身体の動揺さながら船上に立つが如し。

──『断腸亭日乗』

林芙美子(19)　作家
Fumiko Hayashi (19), novelist

(両親の被災状況を確かめるため根津の下宿から新宿まで歩いて向かう時、「危険なので送ってあげる」という青年と出会い、やり取りした場面)

青年は長い事立ち止って汗をふいていたが、洋傘をくるくるまわすとそれを私に突き出していった、

「これで五十銭貸して下さいませんか。」

私はお伽《とぎ》話的なこの青年の行動に好ましい微笑を送った。そして気持ちよく桃色の五十銭札を二枚出して青年の手にのせてやった。

「貴方はお腹がすいてたんですね…」

「ハッハッ…」青年はそうだといってほがらかに哄笑《こうしょう》していた。

「地震って素敵だな!」

──『放浪記』

芥川龍之介(31)　作家
Ryunosuke Akutagawa (31), novelist

(東京・田端の自宅で被災)
午ごろ茶の間にパンと牛乳を喫し了《をは》り、将に茶を飲まんとすれば、忽ち大震の来るあり。(中略)月見橋のほとりに立ち、遥かに東京の天を望めば、天、泥土の色を帯び、焔煙《えんえん》の四方に飛騰《ひとう》するを見る。

——『大震日録』

田山花袋(51)　作家
Katai Tayama (51), novelist

(東京・代々木で被災。その後東京中を見て歩く)
「廃墟」ということは、この大きな自然のリズムではないか。何《ど》んなものにでもいつか一度はやって来るものではないか。(中略)人間の心の中にも絶えず「廃墟」が繰り返されているのではないか。(中略)そして「廃墟」の中から新しい芽が萌え出すのである。

——『東京震災記』

与謝野晶子(44)　歌人
Akiko Yosano (44), poet

(現在の千代田区にあった自宅で被災)
はかなさを常に覚ゆる心にも　今日にまされる日を知らぬかな

——『恐れの中に』

寺田寅彦(44)　物理学者・随筆家
Torahiko Terada (44), physicist and essayist

(上野の喫茶店で知人と会っている最中に被災)
椅子に腰かけている両足のうらを下から木槌で急速に乱打するように感じた。たぶんその前に来たはずの弱い初期微動を気がつかずに直ちに主要動を感じたのだろうという気がして、それにしても妙に短周期の振動だと思っているうちにいよいよ本当の主要動が急激に襲って来た。同時に、これは自分の全く経験のない異常の大地震であると知った。

——『震災日記より』

若山牧水(38)　歌人
Bokusui Wakayama (38), poet

(伊豆・西海岸に滞在中被災)
わがむすめ六つになれるがいたいたし　なゐ*におびえて痩《やせ》の見えたる

——『黒松』

* 地震のこと

※カッコ内の数字は被災当時の年齢。なお、原文の表記等を一部改めたところがあります。

15. 赤坂の倒壊家屋
Collapsed houses in Akasaka

赤坂区(現在の港区)の倒壊家屋が連なる地域。赤坂区では焼失家屋は少なく、犠牲者の多くは圧死によるものだった=1923(大正12)年9月

A row of collapsed houses in Akasaka Ward (present-day Minato Ward). Houses destroyed by fire in the ward were limited in number but many victims were crushed to death. (September 1923)

16. 焼け跡と横浜正金銀行本店の建物
Ruins and Yokohama Specie Bank building

横浜は関東大震災で壊滅的な被害を受けた。一面の焼け野原に外観を残す横浜正金《しょうきん》銀行本店の建物。1階から3階までのほぼ全ての内装と屋上のドームを焼失したが、行員や近くにいた一般人など約340人が建物内の地下室に避難、奇跡的に全員が助かった。現在は神奈川県立歴史博物館になっている＝1923（大正12）年9月

Yokohama suffers catastrophic damage from the quake. In the fire-ravaged area is the Yokohama Specie Bank building whose entire interiors from the first to third floors and rooftop dome were destroyed by fire. About 340 people and bank employees took refuge in the basement and survived. The Kanagawa Prefectural Museum of Cultural History now stands on the site. (September 1923)

17. 大きな被害受けた横浜市電
Seriously damaged Yokohama streetcars

地震の揺れで道路が大きく損傷、車両が取り残された横浜市足曳《あしびき》町（現在の中区）の横浜市電の線路。市電が所有する153両のうち95両が焼失あるいは大破した。変電所も焼失、倒壊し、全線復旧は10月26日になった＝1923（大正12）年9月

The earthquake cracks roads, leaving streetcars abandoned in Yokohama's Ashibiki town (present-day Naka Ward). Ninety-five of 153 city streetcars were destroyed or heavily damaged. The streetcar service was fully restored on Oct. 26. (September 1923)

18. 開港記念横浜会館付近の焼け跡
Charred site near Yokohama Port Opening Memorial Hall

開港記念横浜会館(中央奥、現在の名称は横浜市開港記念会館)付近の焼け跡。横浜開港50周年を記念して1917(大正6)年に開館した会館も時計塔と壁面を残し焼失した。1927(昭和2)年に復旧工事が完了。現在は国の重要文化財に指定され、横浜を代表する歴史的建造物になっている=1923(大正12)年

Ruins around Yokohama Port Opening Memorial Hall (rear center, now called Yokohama City Port Opening Memorial Hall), which opened in 1917 to mark the 50th anniversary of Yokohama port's opening. The hall was destroyed by fire and only its clock tower and murals survived. Restoration work was completed in 1927. It is designated as a national important cultural property and one of Yokohama's major historic landmarks. (1923)

19. 横須賀市内の惨状
Devastation in Yokosuka

横須賀市の高台にある諏訪公園付近から見た市内の惨状。正面の崖部分は大規模に崩落した。関東大震災は相模湾北西部が震源で、震源に近い横須賀市は壊滅的な被害を受けた。丘陵地が多く、崩れた土砂に巻き込まれるなどして大勢が犠牲になった＝1923（大正12）年9月

The devastated port city of Yokosuka, as seen from near Suwa Park. The Great Kanto Earthquake's focus was in northwestern Sagami Bay, and nearby Yokosuka suffered catastrophic damage. Many people lost their lives due to landslides in hilly areas. (September 1923)

20. 横須賀駅付近の崖崩れ
Landslides in Yokosuka

横須賀駅横手の崖崩れ。市街は丘陵に挟まれ、各地で発生した崖崩れで家屋や道路が埋没、大勢の犠牲者が出た＝1923（大正12）年9月

Landslides by Yokosuka Station. The city was sandwiched by hills, and landslides buried houses and roads, causing many casualties. (September 1923)

21. 脱線転覆した列車
Train derails and overturns

神奈川県の大磯付近で脱線転覆した列車。震災による脱線や転覆などの鉄道の被害は震源近くの神奈川県南部が多かった＝1923（大正12）年

A train derails and overturns near Oiso, Kanagawa Prefecture. Many train accidents such as derailments and overturns occurred in southern Kanagawa Prefecture near the earthquake's epicenter. (1923)

22. 倒壊した軍港の食料倉庫
Food warehouse collapses at military port

激震で倒壊した横須賀軍港内のれんが造りの食料倉庫。背後の山も大きく崩れた。横須賀、呉、佐世保などに海軍の拠点となる鎮守府が置かれたが、その中でも横須賀は最大、最重要拠点だった。鎮守府の建物は崩壊、多くの海軍施設も被害を受けたが、海上の艦艇部隊は無傷で、その後の救援活動に大きな力を発揮した＝1923（大正12）年9月

The quake destroys a brick food warehouse at Yokosuka military port and triggers landslides on a nearby mountain. The Imperial Japanese Navy set up naval districts in Yokosuka, Kure and Sasebo, and the Yokosuka unit was the largest and most important. The Yokosuka naval district's buildings collapsed and many naval facilities suffered damage. But the naval fleet at sea was unscratched, playing a vital role in rescue and relief activities. (September 1923)

23. 横須賀の被災地にバラック
Barracks in hard-hit Yokosuka

東京湾に浮かぶ猿島を望む横須賀市の深田町、観念寺町付近（現在の米が浜通付近）。壊滅的な被害を受けた地域だが、バラックが建ち始め、洗濯物が干されている＝1923（大正12）年

Fukada and Kannenji towns (present-day Komegahamadori) in Yokosuka facing Sarushima Island in Tokyo Bay are devastated, prompting construction of barracks. (1923)

24. 被害受けた由比ケ浜
Disaster-hit Yuigahama

関東大震災の揺れによる家屋倒壊、津波、火災による被害を受けた神奈川県鎌倉町（現在の鎌倉市）の由比ケ浜一帯。神奈川県西部、相模湾沿いの逗子市の逗子海岸で約6メートル、小坪地区で約7メートル、鎌倉市の豆腐川流域で約6メートル、藤沢市の引地川流域で約6メートルの津波が押し寄せたという（撮影年月不明、鎌倉市中央図書館提供）

The quake, tsunami and fires devastate Yuigahama beach area in Kamakura town (present-day Kamakura City) in Kanagawa Prefecture. The Zushi coast in Zushi, western Kanagawa Prefecture, along Sagami Bay experienced a tsunami wave of about 6 meters, the Kotsubo district about 7 meters, the Tofu River basin in Kamakura about 6 meters and the Hikiji River basin in Fujisawa also about 6 meters. (Undated, courtesy of Kamakura City Library)

25. 上野公園の西郷像前の被災者
Refugees around Saigo statue in Ueno Park

上野公園の西郷隆盛《さいごうたかもり》像付近の避難者。上野公園一帯は高台に位置し、地震後の火災を免れたため、大勢の人たちの避難場所となった。既存の博物館などの施設も大きな被害を受けず、病院や警察署、臨時の区役所として活用された＝1923（大正12）年9月

Refugees mingle around Saigo Takamori Statue in Ueno Park. Many quake and fire survivors fled to Ueno Park and its vicinity. Damage to museums and other facilities in the park was limited, and they were converted to makeshift hospitals, police stations and ward offices. (September 1923)

26. 上野駅前の被災者
Refugees in front of Ueno Station

家財道具を荷車などに積み避難、上野駅前広場を埋め尽くした人たち。やがてここにも火が入り、上野公園へ逃げ込んだ＝1923（大正12）年9月1日

Many survivors, carrying their belongings by cart, fill the plaza in front of Ueno Station before raging fires forced them to take refuge in Ueno Park. (Sept. 1, 1923)

震災年表　Chronology of Major Earthquakes in Japan over 100 Years

	1923年9月1日　Sept. 1, 1923	1927年3月7日　March 7, 1927
	関東大震災　Great Kanto Earthquake	北丹後地震　North Tango Earthquake
イメージ　Photos		 画像提供：国立科学博
震源　Epicenter	相模湾北西部 Northwestern Sagami Bay	京都府北部 Northern Kyoto Prefecture
最大震度／マグニチュード Maximum Japanese Intensity Scale / Magnitude	6 ／ M7.9	6 ／ M7.3
死者・不明者数　Casualties	105,000人余	2,912人（死者数のみ）
特徴　Characteristics	近代化した首都圏を襲った唯一の巨大地震 The only major earthquake to hit a modern metropolis.	長さ約18kmの郷村断層と、それとほぼ直交する長 7.5kmの山田断層という、2本の共役断層が地表に現れ Two perpendicular faults – the Gomura fault stretc about 18 kilometers and the Yamada fault running a 7.5 km in Kyoto Prefecture – emerged on the surface
トピックス　Key Topics	「暴動を起こす」というデマが広まり、多数の朝鮮人が虐殺された Many Koreans were massacred due to rumors such as Korean uprisings.	

	1948年6月28日　June 28, 1948	1964年6月16日　June 16, 1964
	福井地震　Fukui Earthquake	新潟地震　Niigata Earthquake
イメージ　Photos		
震源　Epicenter	福井県嶺北地方 Reihoku Region in Fukui Prefecture	新潟県沖 Sea of Japan off Niigata Prefecture
最大震度／マグニチュード Maximum Japanese Intensity Scale / Magnitude	6 ／ M7.1	5 ／ M7.5
死者・不明者数　Casualties	3,769人（死者数のみ）	26人（死者数のみ）
特徴　Characteristics	都市直下型地震。戦火から復興途上だった市街地が再び大きな被害を受け、南北に約25kmの断層が生じた An inland earthquake that caused heavy damage to prefectural capital Fukui reeling from damage from the war. It caused a fault extending about 25 kilometers from south to north.	液状化現象で鉄筋コンクリートの建物や橋が被災した Liquefaction phenomena heavily damaged e buildings and bridges made of reinforced concrete.
トピックス　Key Topics	気象庁は1949年1月、新たに震度7を設けた The Japan Meteorological Agency in January 1949 set a new maximum rating of 7 on the Japanese intensity scale, which previously was up to 6.	液状化の対策工法が進むきっかけとなった The disaster promoted the development of architectural methods to cope with liquefaction.

出典

※「震源」および「死者・不明者数」は「理科年表2023国立天文台編（丸善出版）」による（ただし関東大震災の震源は内
府HP「関東大震災100年特設ページ（https://www.bousai.go.jp/kantou100/index.html）」による）

Epicenters and casualties are based on the "Handbook of Scientific Tables 2023, National Observatory of Japan" (Maru
Publishing Co.) The Great Kanto Earthquake's epicenter is based on the Cabinet Office website's special section of
Great Kanto Earthquake's 100th anniversary (https://www.bousai.go.jp/kantou100/index.html).

1933年3月3日　March 3, 1933	1945年1月13日　Jan. 13, 1945	1946年12月21日　Dec. 21, 1946
和三陸地震津波　Showa Sanriku Earthquake and Tsunami	三河地震　Mikawa Earthquake	昭和南海地震　Showa Nankai Earthquake
	 画像提供：愛知県碧南市	
中 anriku Pacific Coast in Northeastern Japan	三河湾　Mikawa Bay in Aichi Prefecture	紀伊半島南方沖 Pacific Waters off Southern Kii Peninsula
M8.1	5 ／ M6.8	5 ／ M8.0
人	2,306人（死者数のみ）	1,330人（死者数のみ）
は少なかったが、津波が三陸沿岸を襲い甚大な被害を らした。波高は綾里湾で28.7mに達した age from the earthquake was limited, but tsunami stated the Sanriku coast and caused extensive ige. Wave height reached 28.7 meters in Ryori Bay, Prefecture.	戦時下であり、援助物資は乏しかったが、緊急輸送路の確保は早く、軍による倒壊家屋の処理等も実施された Relief supplies were poor due to the ongoing World War II, but emergency transportation routes were quickly established and the military also had a hand in dismantling collapsed houses.	津波が静岡県より九州に至る海岸に襲来し三重・徳島・高知沿岸で4～6mに達した Tsunami hit coastal areas from Shizuoka Prefecture in central Japan to Kyushu in the southwest, reaching 4 to 6 meters along coasts in Mie, Tokushima and Kochi prefectures.
	戦時下の災害で、被害報道が厳しく規制された「隠れた地震」 A media blackout was imposed on the wartime disaster which came to be known as “a hidden earthquake” later.	

1995年1月17日　Jan. 17, 1995	2011年3月11日　March 11, 2011	2016年4月16日　April 16, 2016
阪神大震災　Great Hanshin Earthquake	東日本大震災　Great East Japan Earthquake	熊本地震　Kumamoto Earthquake

島付近 nd Awaji Island in Seto Inland Sea	三陸沖 Off Sanriku Pacific Coast in Northeastern Japan	熊本県熊本地方 Kumamoto Region in Kumamoto Prefecture
M7.3	7 ／ M9.0	7 ／ M7.3
人（関連死を含む）	22,312人（関連死を含む）	273人（関連死を含む）
の建物のほか、高速道路、新幹線を含む鉄道路線など壊した。早朝であったため死者の多くは建物の倒壊とによる buildings and expressways as well as Shinkansen other railway lines collapsed. Many people were ned to death or killed by fire due to the predawn lor.	東北地方を中心に沿岸部で津波が発生。東京電力福島第1原発が電源を喪失、炉心溶融や原子炉建屋の水素爆発を起こした The earthquake triggered huge tsunami along coasts in northeastern Japan and other regions. The Fukushima Daiichi nuclear complex of Tokyo Electric Power Co. suffered a loss of electric power, touching off reactor meltdowns and hydrogen explosions.	4月14日に前震、16日に本震があり、熊本県益城町で2回震度7を記録した After a foreshock on April 14, a more powerful earthquake occurred on April 16, registering the maximum rating of 7 on the Japanese intensity scale twice in Mashiki town, Kumamoto Prefecture.
は初動の遅れの指摘を受けて、危機管理を強化した government came under criticism for its delayed response to the disaster and later beefed up crisis agement.		

「最大震度／マグニチュード」は気象庁HP（https://www.data.jma.go.jp/svd/eqev/data/higai/higai-1995.html）による
Maximum Japanese intensity scales and magnitudes are based on the Japan Meteorological Agency’s website (https://www.data.jma.go.jp/svd/eqev/data/higai/higai-1995.html).

第 2 章：暮らしの回復

Chapter 2 : Restoration of Living

27. 鉄管内に避難
Seeking refuge in steel pipes

静岡県小山町の富士紡績の工場で、鉄管内に避難した従業員＝1923（大正12）年9月

Workers seek refuge in steel pipes at Fuji Spinning's Oyama factory in Shizuoka Prefecture. (September 1923)

28. 浅草公園内の避難小屋
Refuge huts in Asakusa Park

浅草公園内に所狭しと並ぶバラックの避難小屋。食べ物屋、果物売りなども。浅草公園は現在の台東区の浅草寺境内一帯＝1923(大正12)年

Numerous barrack huts for disaster refugees fill Asakusa Park (inside the present-day Sensoji Temple in Taito Ward), along with food stalls and fruit vendors. (1923)

ゆであづき
大丼
十銭

29. 宮城外苑に並ぶテント
Tents in Imperial Palace Plaza

宮城《きゅうじょう》外苑（現皇居外苑）に並ぶ避難者のテント。約500張りが用意された。後方中央左に二重橋と伏見櫓《やぐら》、中央右に明治宮殿の屋根が見える＝1923（大正12）年

About 500 tents are set up for refugees in the Imperial Palace Plaza (present-day Imperial Palace Outer Gardens). At rear left are the Nijubashi Bridge and Fushimi turret, and at center right are the roofs of the Meiji Palace. (1923)

30. 保護された迷子
Lost children in protective custody

警視庁の施設に保護された関東大震災による迷子。警視庁は9月20日までに迷子、迷い人1100人以上を保護し、保護者や引き取り人を捜した＝1923（大正12）年

Lost children are under protective custody of the Metropolitan Police Department. The Tokyo police logged more than 1,100 lost children and people under protective custody through Sept. 20 to search for their families and guardians. (1923)

天譴論と船頭小唄

関東大震災が襲った「大正」は政治的にも経済的にも、国際関係上でも大激動、大変革の時代に当たっていた。第一次世界大戦（1914－18年）は日本に棚ぼた式の一時的好況をもたらして「成金」を生み、列強への仲間入り、アジア支配への野望を膨らませた。

国内では近代工業化の急速な進展やロシア革命（1917年）などの影響による労働者階級の自覚と勢力拡大が進み、労働運動、社会運動が激化した。また女性の社会進出と地位向上への目覚ましい活動も見られた。一方で農村では米価暴騰による社会的危機と不安が米騒動を生んだ。都市では百貨店やカフェに象徴される一見華やかな消費社会が出現し、「大衆」が前面に躍り出て、刹那的でどこかはかなく退廃的な文化をけん引した。

大震災の惨状を目の当たりにして「軽はずみで浮ついた世の中を天が罰した」という意味の「天譴《てんけん》論」が唱えられ、その代表格が日本資本主義の父とされる渋沢栄一《しぶさわえいいち》だった。渋沢は「…この文化は果たして道理にかない、天道にかなった文化であったろうか」と疑問を投げ掛けた。

これに対し、その日その日を懸命に生きる下町の庶民、労働者が最も甚大な被害を受けたことを挙げて「なぜこのような人々が罰せられなければならないのか」といった反論が噴出した。

「俺は河原の枯れすすき　同じおまえも枯れすすき　どうせ二人はこの世では花の咲かない枯れすすき」と歌う野口雨情《のぐちうじょう》作詞、中山晋平《なかやましんぺい》作曲による「船頭小唄」は暗さと投げやりな雰囲気を漂わせて人々の心をとらえた。大震災の2年半前に発表され、その後映画化されて爆発的に流行したが、地震後は「あんな歌がはやるから災難を呼んだ」と、天譴論の標的にもなり、一時自粛の動きすらあった。

しかしその後はあらためて盛り上がりを見せ、「逢いたさ見たさに恐さを忘れ」で始まる「籠の鳥」とともに世間から圧倒的に受け入れられた。道徳的正統論と大衆の心情とは別の所にあった。

こうした社会の変容はその裏返しとして、不安と閉塞感を一挙に打開する志向を色濃く持った昭和ファシズムへと導いてゆく。

Divine Punishment Theory & “Sendo Kouta” (Boatman’s Ballad)

The Great Kanto Earthquake occurred during the Taisho Era (1912-1926), a period of great upheaval and transformation politically, economically and diplomatically. World War I (1914-1918) brought about a temporary economic boom in Japan, producing the nouveau riche and heightening the nation’s ambitions to join the great powers and dominate Asia.

Modern industrialization made rapid headway, and the Russian Revolution in 1917 and other factors awakened the working class and its power, intensifying the labor and social movements. There were also noticeable activities toward women’s social advancement and empowerment. But in farming villages, societal crises and anxieties due to soaring rice prices triggered riots among growers of the staple food.

In cities, a superficially glamorous consumer society characterized by the advent of department stores and coffee shops emerged, with the masses coming to the fore to lead an ephemeral and somewhat decadent Japanese culture.

Confronted with the devastations due to the Great Kanto Earthquake, the divine punishment theory that heaven had punished the prevalent insubstantial sentiment of society gained currency. Industrialist Eiichi Shibusawa, dubbed the “father of Japanese capitalism,” championed the theory, questioning whether Japanese culture really made sense and was in a heavenly way.

But the fact that ordinary people and laborers who lived from hand to mouth took the brunt of the disaster led famous intellectuals and others to retort and wonder why they had to be punished.

A gloomy song of apathy called “Sendo Kouta” (Boatman’s Ballad), with lyrics written by Ujo Noguchi and composed by Shimpei Nakayama, caught the minds of many people by sarcastically describing oneself as pampas grass on the riverside. The song was released two and a half years before the earthquake and later made into a blockbuster movie. After the earthquake, however, it became a target of criticism from supporters of the divine punishment theory, temporarily prompting people to refrain from singing popular songs.

But the song later regained popularity and was warmly welcomed by the public, along with another song titled “Kago no Tori” (Bird in Cage) narrating a mistress’s misery. Moral orthodoxy and public mentality were on different wavelengths.

Such social transformation in turn guided the country to fascism in the early Showa Era (1926-1989) with a strong inclination to simultaneously overcome anxiety and a sense of stagnation.

31. 機関車にも鈴なりの人
Evacuees swarm locomotive

田端駅で、先頭の機関車や屋根にも鈴なりになって避難する人たち＝1923（大正12）年9月

Evacuees cluster around locomotive engine at Tabata Station. (September 1923)

32. 避難の汽車を待つ被災者
Survivors wait for evacuation trains

田端駅で避難の汽車を待つ被災者。東北本線では上野駅が焼失、途中の線路上に避難民がいるため日暮里を起点として列車を運転、混雑が予想されるため日暮里と田端双方を発駅にした＝1923（大正12）年9月

Quake survivors wait for evacuation trains at Tabata Station. Ueno Station on the Tohoku Line was destroyed by fire, making Nippori Station an alternative terminal due to the presence of evacuees on the train tracks along the route. Both Nippori and Tabata stations were turned into stopgap terminals due to heavy congestion. (September 1923)

33. 横浜駅から避難する人たち
Escaping from Yokohama Station

倒壊は免れたが、外壁を残し駅舎が焼失した横浜駅から、屋根がない貨車で避難する人たち。東海道本線は重要路線のため応急復旧工事が急がれ9月8日には横浜―人船間が開通して、品川―人船間の旅客列車が運行された＝1923（大正12）年9月

Evacuees flee on roofless freight car from Yokohama Station whose building was destroyed by fire. Frantic restoration work on the vital Tokaido Line helped to reopen the train service between Yokohama and Ofuna on Sept. 8, and passenger trains also resumed running between Shinagawa and Ofuna. (September 1923)

34. 鉄橋を歩いて渡る人たち
People cross railway bridge

東海道線は大船以西は被害が激しく、土砂崩れがあった神奈川県の山北《やまきた》—谷《や》峨《が》間（現在はＪＲ御殿場線）の第三酒《さか》匂《わ》川《がわ》鉄橋を歩いて渡る人たち。この区間の復旧は10月28日だった＝1923（大正12）年9月

Damage to the Tokaido Line in areas west of Ofuna is heavy, prompting people to walk across No. 3 Sakawagawa railway bridge between Yamakita and Yaga stations (presently on the JR Gotemba Line) in Kanagawa Prefecture. The suspended section was restored on Oct. 28. (September 1923)

35. 線路沿いの山道を歩く人たち
People trek mountain road along train tracks

関東大震災で鉄道路線は大きな被害を受けた。東海道線は各地で寸断、不通となった神奈川県の山北―谷峨間(現在はＪＲ御殿場線)の線路沿いの山道を歩いて移動する人たち。左は酒匂川。この状況は10月28日に復旧するまで続いた＝1923(大正12)年

Quake causes heavy damage to train networks, disrupting train services on the Tokaido Line in many regions and forcing people to walk along train tracks between Yamakita and Yaga stations (presently on the JR Gotemba Line). Train service between the two sections resumed on Oct. 28. (1923)

36. 焼け落ちた万世橋駅
Manseibashi Station burnt down

赤れんが造りの万世橋駅(現在の千代田区神田須田町)は壁を残して焼け落ちた。万世橋駅は東京駅の赤れんが駅舎と同じく辰野金吾が設計、1912(明治45)年に中央線ターミナル駅として開業した。中央の銅像は日露戦争の「軍神」広瀬武夫《ひろせたけお》中佐と杉野孫七《すぎのまごしち》兵曹長＝1923(大正12)年9月

Redbrick Manseibashi Station (presently in Kanda-Suda, Chiyoda Ward) is destroyed by fire. Designed by architect Kingo Tatsuno who also designed the redbrick Tokyo Station, Manseibashi Station opened as the Chuo Line's terminal in 1912. In the middle are the bronze statues of Takeo Hirose, an Imperial Japanese Navy officer deified as a "military god" for his heroism in the Russo-Japanese War, and another hero, Chief Warrant Officer Magoshichi Sugino. (September 1923)

37. 仲見世の焼け跡
Nakamise shopping street in ruins

浅草寺の参道沿いに並ぶ仲見世の焼け跡。各店はれんが造りだったが壊滅した＝1923（大正12）年

A quake-triggered fire leaves in ruins the Nakamise shopping street dotted with brick shops on the approach to Sensoji Temple. (1923)

関東大震災時の虐殺事件

関東大震災は自然災害として未曽有の被害をもたらすと同時に社会的混乱を生み出した。民族差別意識やイデオロギー対立などを背景に理不尽な虐殺事件が地震直後から続発した。真相をめぐる謎は今も残る。

【朝鮮人大虐殺】

1923年9月1日の関東大震災発生直後から、壊滅状態となった東京や神奈川を中心に「朝鮮人が暴動を起こす」「井戸に毒を入れた」などのデマ、流言が広がり、警察や軍隊、竹やりなどで武装した民間の自警団が韓国・朝鮮人を無差別に虐殺した。

正確な被害実態は今も不明だが、政府の中央防災会議の報告書によると、震災による死者約10万5000人の1〜数%が虐殺犠牲者とされ、6000人以上が死亡したという調査結果もある。中国人や、間違えられた日本人も犠牲になった。

毎年9月1日には東京都墨田区の都立横網町公園で朝鮮人追悼式典が営まれ、発生100年の前日に当たる2023年8月31日には文京区で1800人規模の追悼大会が開催される。韓国の政界でも真相解明や被害者の名誉回復を求める声が上がっている。

【甘粕事件(大杉栄事件)】

9月16日、憲兵大尉の甘粕正彦《あまかすまさひこ》らがアナキストの主要人物であった大杉栄《おおすぎさかえ》と妻伊藤野枝《いとうのえ》、6歳のおいの3人を憲兵隊本部に拉致して殺害した。大震災の混乱に乗じてアナキストらが不穏な動きを起こすのを憂慮した犯行とされた。軍法会議で甘粕に懲役10年などの判決が下ったが真相は糾明されず、甘粕はその後恩赦で釈放された。

【亀戸事件】

9月3日から4日にかけて、東京・亀戸警察署が以前から労働争議で敵対関係にあった社会主義者の川合義虎《かわいよしとら》ら10人を捕らえて留置。川合らは軍に引き渡され、刺殺された。震災の約3カ月前には、共産党員30余人が警察により一斉検挙されていた。

38. 憲兵隊の古井戸
Old well at Kenpeitai military police

憲兵隊大尉の甘粕正彦らが大杉栄と妻の伊藤野枝、6歳のおいを東京・大手町の東京憲兵隊本部に拉致、3日後、3人の遺体は構内の古井戸(中央のれんが積み部分の下)から見つかった＝1923(大正12)年

Masahiko Amakasu, a lieutenant in Kenpeitai military police, and his officers hauled off anarchists Sakae Osugi, his wife Noe Ito and his 6-year-old nephew to Tokyo Kenpeitai headquarters in the Otemachi district on Sept. 16. Their bodies were found three days later in an old well (below a pile of bricks in the center). (1923)

Massacre after Great Kanto Earthquake

The Great Kanto Earthquake caused unprecedented damage as a natural calamity as well as social confusion. Outrageous mass killings frequently took place immediately after the earthquake against the backdrop of ethnic discrimination and ideological rifts. The truths behind the atrocities have yet to be uncovered.

【Massacre of Koreans】

Soon after the Great Kanto Earthquake, rumors such as Korean uprisings and poisoning of wells by Koreans spread mainly in Tokyo and Kanagawa Prefecture, prompting the police, military and vigilante groups armed with bamboo spears and other weapons to indiscriminately kill Korean residents. The exact death toll is not clear to this day, but a report by the governmental Central Disaster Prevention Council says that up to several percent of the roughly 105,000 fatalities from the quake were massacre victims, while other studies put the number at more than 6,000. Among the victims were also Chinese and Japanese who were mistaken for Koreans.

An annual memorial service is held for the Korean victims in Yokoamicho Park in Tokyo's Sumida Ward on Sept. 1 every year. A centennial ceremony to remember the victims is set for Aug. 31, 2023, in Tokyo's Bunkyo Ward, with about 1,800 people in attendance. There have been calls within the South Korean political community to unearth the truth and restore the honor of the Korean victims.

【Amakasu Incident(Sakae Osugi Incident)】

On Sept. 16, 1923, Masahiko Amakasu, a lieutenant in the Kenpeitai military police, and his officers arrested and murdered key anarchists Sakae Osugi and his wife Noe Ito, along with his 6-year-old nephew. They killed the trio ostensibly for fear that anarchists and others would incite disturbances to take advantage of the earthquake. Amakasu was court-martialed and sentenced to 10 years in prison. But the incident was not fully probed, and Amakasu was freed after three years due to a general amnesty.

【Kameido Incident】

From Sept. 3 to 4, 1923, police in charge of Tokyo's Kameido area arrested and detained Yoshitora Kawai and nine other social activists with whom they had long-running confrontations over labor disputes. The activists were turned over to the military and stabbed to death. About three months earlier, over 30 Japanese Communist Party members had been rounded up.

39. 朝鮮人犠牲者を追悼
Remembering Korean victims

東京都墨田区の横網町公園で、関東大震災朝鮮人犠牲者追悼碑に献花する人たち＝2020(令和2)年9月1日

People lay flowers at a ceremony in Yokoamicho Park in Tokyo's Sumida Ward for Korean massacre victims in the aftermath of the quake and ensuing fires. (Sept. 1, 2020)

40. 宮内省の医療班
Medical contingent from Imperial Household Ministry

被災者収容施設などを巡回する宮内省(現宮内庁)巡回救療班(撮影場所不明)。婦人科、小児科などの医師、薬剤師、看護婦(看護師)などから構成、無料で被災者の診療を行った＝1923(大正12)年9月

Members of a medical relief contingent from the Imperial Household Ministry (present-day Imperial Household Agency) patrol shelters for disaster survivors. These medical personnel included gynecologists, pediatricians, pharmacists and nurses. Treatment was free. (September 1923)

41. 米国救護班のテント病院
U.S. makeshift hospitals

麻布の高松宮御用地に設置される米国救護班のテント野外病院。米国は横浜にも病院を建設、国籍を問わず傷病者を治療した。高松宮御用地は現在、港区の有栖川宮記念公園になっている＝1923（大正12）年

U.S. relief team members set up makeshift hospitals at Prince Takamatsu's residence in Tokyo's Azabu district. The U.S. also established makeshift hospitals in Yokohama to treat disaster survivors regardless of nationality. The Prince Takamatsu residence is now Arisugawa-no-miya Memorial Park in Minato Ward. (1923)

42. 中華民国の赤十字隊救護団
Red Cross relief team from Republic of China

中華民国の赤十字隊救護団の看護婦ら（撮影場所不明）。同国は医療支援チーム派遣とともに多額の義援金集めや大量の食料支援も行った＝1923（大正12）年

Nurses of a Red Cross relief mission from then Republic of China are at work. The ROC also raised funds and provided food assistance. (1923)

関東大震災で寄せられた海外からの義援金品 合計　4157万1000円（現在の価値で1000億円超相当）		
1	米国	3093万1000円
2	英国	578万円
3	中華民国	260万円
4	フランス	45万1000円
5	オランダ	42万3000円
6	ブラジル	30万6000円
7	ベルギー	22万9000円
8	ペルー	19万9000円
9	メキシコ	13万8000円
10	イタリア	8万8000円

※東京市（当時）の資料による

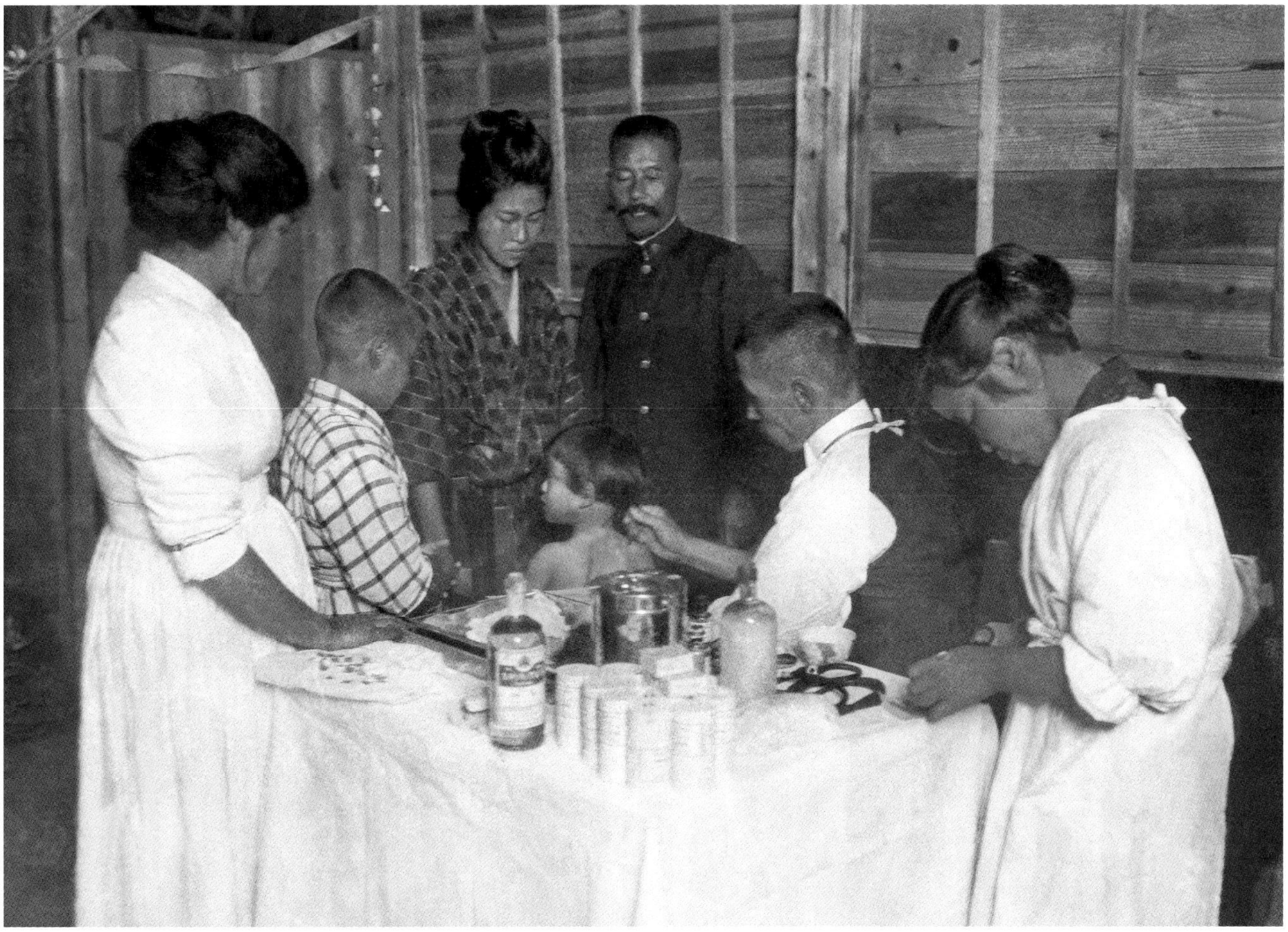

43. 被災者の無料診療
Free medical treatment

被災者の無料診療（撮影場所不明）。東京市内には各種救護班が展開した。警視庁や市、日本赤十字社、地方公共団体の医療班、各地の大学病院などにより広範かつ組織的に行われた＝1923（大正12）年

Various relief teams in Tokyo carry out free medical treatment for disaster survivors. Involved in such large-scale relief activities were the Metropolitan Police Department, city offices, the Japanese Red Cross, and medical teams from local public entities and university hospitals. (1923)

44. 貞明皇后が被災病児らを慰問
Empress Teimei visits children

日本赤十字社病院(現在の渋谷区の日本赤十字社医療センター)で、被災病児らを慰問する貞明皇后(左から3人目、大正天皇の皇后)。皇后は12月まで、東京や横浜の病院、避難者収容施設を見舞った=1923(大正12)年9月30日

Empress Teimei (wife of Emperor Taisho, 3rd from L) consoles children at Japanese Red Cross Hospital (present-day Japanese Red Cross Medical Center in Shibuya Ward). She also visited other hospitals and shelters in Tokyo and Yokohama through December. (Sept. 30, 1923)

45. 支援物資の陸揚げ作業
Unloading relief supplies

海上輸送された救援物資の陸揚げ作業が続く芝浦（現在の港区）。当時の東京港は水深が浅く、大型の救援船が接岸できる設備がなかった。唯一芝浦の水深がある場所で陸揚げができたが、揚陸地の不整備や作業担当者の熟練不足などで、沖合は救援船が混み合う状態だった＝1923（大正12）年

Workers unload relief supplies in Shibaura district (present-day Minato Ward). The water depth at Tokyo port was shallow at the time, preventing large relief ships from anchoring. Shibaura was the only place for unloading relief supplies, but insufficient unloading infrastructure and unskilled staff caused an offshore congestion of relief ships. (1923)

46. 芝浦に着いた救援物資
Relief supplies arrive in Shibaura

海上輸送され芝浦（現在の港区）に着いた食料や救援物資を運ぶ兵士たち。救援物資は海軍が海上輸送から陸揚げ作業を、陸軍が陸揚げ地点から東京府、市が希望する配給所までの運搬を担った＝1923（大正12）年

Soldiers carry food and relief supplies in Shibaura (present-day Minato Ward). The Imperial Japanese Navy unloaded relief supplies, and the Army transported them to distribution centers designated by Tokyo Prefecture and city offices. (1923)

47. 被災地で活動する軍隊
Military in relief operations

赤坂区（現在の港区）の倒壊した建物と移動する軍の車両。関東大震災では陸軍が約5万人、海軍が約3万7000人態勢で救援活動に当たった＝1923（大正12）年9月

Military vehicles run along collapsed buildings in Akasaka Ward (present-day Minato Ward). About 50,000 members of the Imperial Japanese Army and about 37,000 Navy personnel participated in post-quake relief activities. (September 1923)

48. 尋ね人などの案内所
Notices for missing persons

尋ね人や行き先案内など、各種情報の拠点となる東京市内の案内所を訪れた大勢の人たち。救援活動は官公署ばかりでなく、各種団体、町内会、退役した軍人らの在郷軍人会などボランティアによっても担われた＝1923（大正12）年

People flock to information outposts for missing persons and destination guidance. Such relief activities were conducted by municipalities, various groups, neighborhood associations and members of war veteran groups. (1923)

49. 無料電車に鈴なりの人
Free riders cling to streetcar

火災による被害が大きかった東京市電。部分運転を再開した当初は運賃無料で、麹町区有楽町（現在の千代田区）の警視庁前を走る電車には鈴なりの人たちが。11月下旬に深川方面を除き大部分の運行を再開、全線での復旧は約1年後だった＝1923（大正12）年9月

Tokyo's streetcar system is heavily damaged by fire. It partially resumed service free of charge, attracting free riders on the streetcar running in front of the Tokyo Metropolitan Police Department in Yurakucho, Kojimachi Ward (present-day Chiyoda Ward). Its near full-scale operations restarted in late November, except in the Fukagawa-bound area, with its service fully restored about one year later. (September 1923)

50. 桜木町駅の張り紙
Notices at Sakuragicho Station

焼失した横浜市の桜木町駅前に張られた尋ね人や避難先、告知などが書かれた紙。通信や郵便などの連絡手段が絶たれた被災地では、駅や派出所、焼け残った建物など多くの人が通る場所への張り紙が「伝言板」となった＝1923（大正12）年

Patches of paper about missing persons and places of refuge and other notices are plastered in front of Sakuragicho Station. In disaster-hit areas, where telecommunication, postal and other means of getting in touch with one another were lost, such patches of paper were posted at railway stations, police boxes and the remains of burned buildings as message boards. (1923)

山梨県人へ
急告
内外科醫士
招聘
(優待)
神奈川方面警備隊司令部
荒井伊八
大津町

51. 被災地の洋服店
Apparel shop in Yokosuka

大きな被害を受けた横須賀で、倒壊を免れた洋服店の前で売られる衣料品＝1923(大正12)年9月

An apparel shop in heavily damaged Yokosuka sells clothing outdoors. (September 1923)

52. 路上の食べ物売り
Roadside food stall

れんが造りの建物前の路上で調理する人たちと客（撮影場所不明）。関東大震災後には天ぷらやおでんなどとともに、簡単に提供できるすいとん（小麦粉に水を加え、こねてからちぎり、汁で煮たもの）を売る店が数多くできた＝1923（大正12）年9月

A roadside food stall attracts customers at an unknown location in the quake's aftermath. There were many stalls selling tempura, oden (hot pot dish) and easily prepared flour dumplings boiled in soup. (September 1923)

53. 芝増上寺門前の物売り
Food vendors in front of Zojoji Temple

芝増上寺の門前の物売り。野菜天ぷら、すいとんが1杯10銭。ゆ で小豆なども売られくいた。増上寺は，同じ芝区（現在の港区）にあ った芝離宮とともに公設バラックの大規模な建設場所となった＝1923（人正12）年9月

Food vendors sell vegetable tempura, flour dumplings boiled in soup and boiled red beans in front of Zojoji Temple in Shiba Ward (present-day Minato Ward). The temple accommodated many public barracks for evacuees, along with Shiba Rikyu Garden. (September 1923)

54. 銀行に並ぶ人たち
Lining up at Tokyo bank

本郷（現在の文京区）の東京貯蔵銀行支店で預金の引き出しに並ぶ人たち。関東大震災で銀行も大打撃を受け、被災地の銀行は震災直後からほとんどが休業していた。9月7日に政府の支払い猶予令が公布され、東京では8日以降業務が再開された＝1923（大正12）年

People line up at a Tokyo Chozo (savings) Bank branch in Hongo (present-day Bunkyo Ward) to withdraw their money. Banks in quake-hit areas halted their operations. The government announced a moratorium notice on Sept. 7, and banking operations in Tokyo resumed on Sept. 8 and thereafter. (1923)

55. 銀座の焼け跡の古着屋
Outdoor second-hand shop in Ginza

れんがなど、がれきが残る銀座の焼け跡で店を開く古着屋。不燃化を目指して造られたれんが造りの家屋が並んだ西欧風の銀座の街並みも、火災により失われてしまった＝1923（大正12）年

An old-clothesman operates in Ginza littered with rubble. (1923)

56. 自転車のパンク修理屋
Puncture repair shop

神田須田町(現在の千代田区)の自転車のパンク修理屋。散乱するごみなどでパンクが急増、大繁盛した＝1923(大正12)年

A puncture repair shop operator in Kanda-Suda (presently in Chiyoda Ward). Streets were littered with garbage, causing frequent flat tires and keeping repair shop operators busy. (1923)

57. 浅草寺の物売り
Peddlers at Sensoji Temple

関東大震災で焼け残った浅草寺の宝蔵門前の物売りと行き交う人たち。震災は浅草区（現在の台東区東部）の96%を焼失させた。大勢の人たちが避難した浅草寺周辺がかろうじて残った=1923（大正12）年

Peddlers and pedestrians in front of Sensoji Temple's Hozomon gate. Ninety-six percent of Asakusa Ward (presently eastern Taito Ward) was destroyed by fire, forcing many people to flee to Sensoji Temple and its vicinity. (1923)

58. 冠水した道路歩く女性
Women walk flooded roads

大雨で冠水した深川区（現在の江東区北部）の道路を、着物の裾を持って歩く人たち＝1923（大正12）年
Women in kimono wade through flooded roads in Fukagawa Ward (presently northern Koto Ward). (1923)

59. 冠水した道路を馬車で移動
Traveling by carriage

深川区（現在の江東区北部）猿江町で、大雨により冠水した道路を馬車で移動する人たち。東京湾岸部の干拓地や埋め立て地では地盤が液状化、陥没や地割れ、建物の沈下、傾斜などが起きた＝1923（大正12）年

People ride horse-drawn carriages on flooded roads in Sarue, Fukagawa Ward (presently northern Koto Ward). Reclaimed land and landfills triggered liquefaction, cave-ins and cracks, causing building subsidence and tilts. (1923)

60. 水に漬かって商売
Vendor on flooded roads

大雨により冠水した本所、深川方面(現在の墨田区、江東区)の道路に食器類を並べた店。震災後、雨のたびに広い地域が水に漬かった＝1923(大正12)年

A tableware vendor defies flooding to do business in Honjo and Fukagawa areas (presently Sumida and Koto wards). (1923)

61. 水に漬かり配給待つ
Waiting for food rations in floods

台風で水に漬かった本所区（現在の墨田区南部）のバラック街でバケツを手に配給を受ける被災者＝1923（大正12）年

People receive food rations with buckets in hand in flooded Honjo Ward (present-day southern Sumida Ward). (1923)

62. 陸軍工兵隊の市電撤去作業
Removing charred streetcars

焼けて骨組みだけになった東京市電の車体の撤去作業をする陸軍工兵隊（撮影場所不明）。工兵隊は鉄道連隊などと協力して電車橋・軌道の復旧に従事した＝1923（大正12）年9月

Imperial Japanese Army corps of engineers remove charred Tokyo streetcars at an unknown location. The army engineers worked with railroad regiments and others to repair streetcar bridges and restore tracks. (1923)

63. 海軍電信隊の復旧工事
Navy telegraph corps in restoration work

芝区琴平町（現在の港区虎ノ門）付近で通信線の復旧工事をする海軍電信隊。関東大震災では東京市内の郵便局、電信局、電話局のほとんどが焼失、倒壊して通信機関としての機能が果たせなくなった＝1923（大正12）年9月

Members of Japanese Imperial Navy telegraph corps are engaged in restoration work near Kotohira in Shiba Ward (present-day Toranomon, Minato Ward). Fires destroyed or crippled most postal, telegraph and telephone offices in Tokyo, incapacitating their communications functions. (September 1923)

64. マスク売り
Face mask seller

日比谷公園で1枚5銭のマスクを売る人。暑さが残る季節で、粉じんや悪臭対策に必要だった＝1923（大正12）年

A woman sells face masks in Hibiya Park to protect against dust and foul smells amid lingering summer heat. (1923)

（上段写真左から）

65. 地震で折れた浅草の凌雲閣
Ryounkaku tower collapses

浅草のランドマークだった展望塔「凌雲閣」（通称・浅草十二階）。関東大震災で建物の8階部分から上が折れる形で倒壊した＝1923（大正12）年9月

Ryounkaku tower (commonly called Asakusa 12 Stories). Quake destroys upper floors of Ryounkaku tower, an Asakusa landmark. (1923)

66. 爆破される凌雲閣
Ryounkaku tower faces demolition

地震で8階部分から上が崩壊したため陸軍工兵隊が爆破。1回で爆破し切れなかった。左奥には地震被害も火災も免れた浅草寺の五重塔などが見える＝1923（大正12）年9月23日

Imperial Japanese Army corps of engineers try to demolish Ryounkaku tower with explosives. Rear left is Sensoji Temple's five-story pagoda. (September 23, 1923)

67. 2回目の爆破
2nd try at demolition

1回目の爆破で残った部分を再爆破した＝1923（大正12）年9月23日

Army engineers make a second attempt to demolish the remains of Ryounkaku tower. (September 23, 1923)

68. そびえ立つ凌雲閣（被災前）
Ryounkaku tower (before the quake)

震災が起こる前の凌雲閣。エレベーターを備えた、当時では珍しい高層建築だった（撮影年不明）

Ryounkaku tower, a rare skyscraper equipped with an elevator system, in Asakusa Park. (undated)

69. 爆破準備する陸軍工兵隊
Army engineers prepare to blow up dangerous buildings

危険建物の爆破準備をする陸軍工兵隊（撮影場所不明）。れんがや石、コンクリートなどで造られた、関東大震災で焼失した建物の残骸除去は大変な作業で、復興の障害となった。東京市内では大蔵省（現財務省）、逓信省（当時郵便や通信などを管轄）、浅草の凌雲閣など約50カ所が爆破され、残骸除去が進むことになった＝1923（大正12）年

Imperial Japanese Army corps of engineers prepare to blow up a partially damaged building made of bricks, stones and concrete at an unknown location. Such debris hampered restoration work. Army engineers conducted demolition work at about 50 locations, including the Finance Ministry, Communications Ministry and Ryounkaku tower. (1923)

70. 米国大使館の焼け跡
U.S. Embassy in ruins

赤坂区榎坂町（現在の港区赤坂）の米国大使館の焼け跡でがれきなどを片付ける米兵。米国大使館、公使館として1890（明治23）年から使われていた木造建築物が焼失、仮事務所を震災に耐えた帝国ホテルに開設した＝1923（大正12）年9月

U.S. soldiers clean up debris at the charred U.S. Embassy. A wooden building housing the U.S. Embassy burned down, and a temporary U.S. diplomatic mission was set up inside the Imperial Hotel. (September 1923)

71. 危険建物の取り壊し
Dismantling dangerous structure

関東大震災で倒壊、一部が残った東京電灯の浅草発電所（現在の台東区）の人力による取り壊し作業。震災後、千住に火力発電所が新設された＝1923（大正12）年

Workers manually dismantle a power station in Asakusa (present-day Taito Ward) of Tokyo Dento. Tokyo Dento built a thermal power station in Senju after the quake. (1923)

72. 摂政宮が焼け跡視察

Crown Prince Hirohito inspects damage

上野公園内の被害状況を視察する摂政宮(中央右の馬上手前、後の昭和天皇)。摂政宮は馬に乗り神田、京橋、日本橋の焼け跡を回り、上野公園の高台からは市内を眺望、永《なが》田《た》秀《ひで》次《じ》郎《ろう》東京市長らから被害状況の説明を受けた＝1923(大正12)年9月15日

Horse-riding Crown Prince Hirohito (later Emperor Showa, center right) checks charred areas in Kanda, Kyobashi and Nihombashi. On a hill at Ueno Park, he received a briefing on quake damage from Tokyo Mayor Hidejiro Nagata. (Sept. 15, 1923)

73. 築地本願寺で配給待つ人の列
Waiting for rations at Tsukiji Honganji Temple

京橋区（現在の中央区南部）の築地本願寺焼け跡で配給される食料を求めて並ぶ被災者の長い列＝1923（大正12）年

People queue up for food rations in Tsukiji Honganji Temple in Kyobashi Ward (presently southern Chuo Ward). (1923)

74. 食料配給所に並ぶ被災者
Disaster victims at food distribution center

京橋区(現在の中央区南部)の築地本願寺に設けられた配給所で、米を受け取るため並ぶ被災者=1923(大正12)年

Disaster victims line up at a ward food distribution center in Tsukiji Honganji Temple in Kyobashi Ward (presently southern Chuo Ward). (1923)

75. 犠牲者に供える花を売る人
Selling flowers to mourn victims

約3万8000人が炎に包まれて命を落とした陸軍被服廠（軍服などを作る工場）跡地（現在の墨田区横網）で、犠牲者に供える花を売る人たち＝1923（大正12）年

Young people sell flowers at the former Imperial Japanese Army Clothing Depot (presently Yokoami, Sumida Ward), where an estimated 38,000 people were killed in fire whirls triggered by a firestorm after taking refuge in the depot. (1923)

76. 被服廠跡で供養
Mourning at army clothing depot

陸軍被服廠跡を訪れ、犠牲者の供養をする大勢の人たち。後方には犠牲者のお骨の山が見える＝1923（大正12）年9月

Mourners flock to the former Imperial Japanese Army Clothing Depot. In the rear is a mountain of bones and ashes of those killed in fire whirls triggered by a firestorm after taking refuge in the depot. (September 1923)

77. バラック電話交換局
Barrack telephone exchange

日比谷に建てられたバラックの電話交換局。関東大震災による火災で東京、横浜などでは多くの電話局、電話線などが焼失した。当時、一般家庭へは普及していなかったが、各行政機関の情報伝達網はほぼ壊滅した＝1923（大正12）年

A barrack telephone exchange in Hibiya. Many telephone exchanges and cables in Tokyo and Yokohama were destroyed by fire after the quake, obliterating communications networks among administrative entities. (1923)

78. 仮設の日比谷警察署
Makeshift Hibiya Police Station

仮の建物に看板を掲げた日比谷警察署。関東大震災では警視庁の日比谷庁舎に加え、市部に置かれていた警察署40のうち21が焼失、焼失を免れた署も多くが損壊した＝1923（大正12）年

A building bears makeshift Hibiya Police Station's name. The Metropolitan Police Department's Hibiya building and 21 police stations in the city were destroyed by fire, and many others suffered extensive damage. (1923)

79. 日比谷公園の臨時公設市場

Temporary public market

日比谷公園内の臨時公設市場。下関から鮮魚が届いたとの紙が張られ、しょうゆ、みそ、砂糖、缶詰なども並ぶ＝1923（大正12）年

A temporary public market in Hibiya Park. A notice on the arrival of fresh fish from Shimonoseki in western Japan was posted, and soy sauce, miso, sugar and canned goods were also on sale. (1923)

80. 仮設の青物市場
Makeshift vegetable market

震災で壊滅したが直ちに仮設で開場し、秋物野菜が並ぶ神田多町（現在の千代田区）の青物市場。その後、1928（昭和3）年には秋葉原西北に、89（平成元）年には大田区へと移転した＝1923（大正12）年9月

A makeshift vegetable market opens in Kanda-Tacho (presently in Chiyoda Ward) to sell autumn vegetables. The market was later relocated to the northwest of Akihabara in 1928 and Ota Ward in 1989. (September 1923)

81. 日本橋から移転した芝浦の魚市場
Fish market relocated to Shibaura from Nihombashi

日本橋から移転した芝浦（現在の港区）の仮設の魚市場では樺太（現在のロシア極東サハリン）からのサケが荷揚げされた。しかし仮市場は交通の便が悪く、狭いなどの理由から12月には築地の海軍省用地に移転した＝1923（大正12）年9月17日

Salmon from Karafuto (present-day Sakhalin in far eastern Russia) are unloaded at a temporary fish market in Shibaura (present-day Minato Ward), which was relocated from Nihombashi. The fish market was relocated again to a Navy Ministry site in Tsukiji in December because the Shibaura market was inconvenient and small. (Sept. 17, 1923)

82. にぎり飯作り
Making rice balls

大勢の人たちが避難生活を送る上野公園で、被災児童に配るにぎり飯を作る日本女子大卒業生の会のメンバー。市内の各大学も避難場所の提供、医療活動、衣類や食事の提供など多岐にわたる救援活動を実施した＝1923（大正12）年10月

Members of Japan Women's University alumnae group make rice balls for children living in Ueno Park shelters. Other universities and colleges in Tokyo also provided shelters, participated in medical activities and offered clothes and meals. (October 1923)

83. 無料の散髪
Free haircut

大勢の人たちが避難生活を送る浅草公園で、無料の散髪をしてもらう被災者＝1923（大正12）年

An evacuee in Asakusa Park has his hair cut for free. (1923)

84. 巡回風呂
Mobile bath makes rounds

巡回風呂で久しぶりに体を流す子どもたち（撮影場所不明）。当時は焼け跡の水たまりや池で行水する人たちもいた＝1923（大正12）年9月

Children enjoy mobile bath service at an unidentified location. Post-quake photos included those of people washing themselves in puddles and ponds. (September 1923)

85. 公園内の野外学校
Outdoor school in Hibiya Park

日比谷公園内にござを敷き、被災児童らを対象に少年団日本連盟が主宰した「野外少国民学校」。少国民(小学生)を対象に市内6カ所に設置、9月20日ごろから、10月上旬まで続けられた。関東大震災では東京市立小学校195校のうち118校が焼失した。学校再開後もテントやバラックも教室として使われ、露天での授業、二部授業なども行われた=1923(大正12)年9月

In Hibiya Park, children attend an outdoor school organized by Boy Scouts of Japan. Six such outdoor classes for elementary schoolchildren operated from around Sept. 20 to early October. After the quake, 118 of 195 city-run public elementary schools were destroyed by fire. Even after public schools reopened, tents and barracks were used as classrooms, and outdoor and two-shift classes were held. (September 1923)

86. バラック前で遊ぶ子ども
Playing in front of barracks

日比谷公園のバラック前で遊ぶ子どもたち。バラックは被災者の収容施設として警視庁、東京府、市、区、富豪、民間団体などにより、公園や小学校の焼け跡などに建てられた。一方、バラックの絶対数が足りず、多くの被災者は自力で焼け跡に仮小屋を建てた＝1923（大正12）年

Children play in front of barracks in Hibiya Park. The Metropolitan Police Department, City of Tokyo, other cities and wards, wealthy people and private groups built such barracks for evacuees. Shortages of barracks forced some disaster survivors to build makeshift huts on the sites of their ruined houses. (1923)

大風呂敷と呼ばれた男の復興計画―関東大震災と後藤新平

関東大震災直後、主に軍部から東京遷都論が出た。防災、国防上の観点などから条件不利な東京からの遷都が提唱され、朝鮮半島や兵庫県が候補地に挙げられた。アジア支配の目論見も透けて見える案だった。しかし内務大臣後藤新平《ごとうしんぺい》を含む政府、有力者らの反対ですぐに立ち消えとなった。

後藤は台湾民政長官、南満州鉄道初代総裁、逓信大臣、外務大臣などを歴任。震災の3年前に東京市長となり、東京の都市改造に意欲を見せていた。震災が起きると山本権兵衛首相は後藤を内相に迎えて震災復興の責任者とした。帝都復興審議会と帝都復興院が設置され、後藤は復興院総裁に就任した。

後藤は東京改造の絶好の機会と捉え、「帝都復興案」を急ぎ作らせた。それによると、焼土のすべてを公債の発行により買い上げ、大規模な道路整備や土地区画を整理して欧米式の大都市建設を実現するなどとした。最初の案では国家予算の2倍にあたる30億円を要するともいわれた。

そのあまりにも大胆な計画は「後藤の大風呂敷」と評され、政争も絡んでその後予算を数億円規模にまで削られて幻に終わり、復興院も廃止された。山本内閣は1923(大正12)年に起きた皇太子裕仁(後の昭和天皇)に対する発砲事件(虎ノ門事件)の責任を取って総辞職し、後藤も内相を退いた。

実際の復興は復興院を引き継いだ内務省復興局や東京市が担った。23年中には東海道線が全線復旧、築地の魚河岸が開場。24(大正13)年には東京市営バスが開設、同愛記念病院財団が設立、鉄筋コンクリート造りの同潤会アパートが建設に着手した。その他、銀座に市電復活、隅田川の永代橋完成、横浜の桟橋回復、がれきの埋め立てで山下公園完成などと急ピッチで進んだ。

モータリゼーションを先取りした防災機能を持つ大幅員の幹線道路建設のほか、上下水道、都市ガスなどの生活インフラの整備も手掛けられた。後藤の計画はそのままでは実現しなかったが、江戸時代以来の木造建築密集都市だった東京が近代都市に生まれ変わる基礎をつくり、現在に続いている。

帝都復興事業完成を祝う式典が30(昭和5)年3月、皇居・二重橋前で開かれた。しかし後藤はそれを見ることなく前年に世を去った。

87. 後藤新平
Shimpei Goto

逓信相、内相、外相、東京放送局(現在のNHK)総裁などを歴任した(撮影年不明)

Shimpei Goto held such posts as communications minister, home minister and foreign minister, as well as head of Tokyo Broadcasting Station, a precursor to public broadcaster NHK.

Great Kanto Earthquake & Reconstruction Plan by Man with a Tall Tale - Shimpei Goto

Immediately after the Great Kanto Earthquake, debate on relocating the Japanese capital from Tokyo ensued, mainly in the military. Proposals were made to quit disadvantageous Tokyo from the standpoint of national defense, and the Korean Peninsula and Hyogo Prefecture in the west emerged as candidate sites. Behind the idea was a move viewed as a plot to achieve Asian domination. But these proposals were quickly dismissed due to opposition from government officials, including Home Minister Shimpei Goto, and other influential figures.

Goto served as the first civil administrator under the governor-general of Taiwan, president of South Manchuria Railway, and home minister and foreign minister, among other posts. He became Tokyo mayor in 1920 and signaled his eagerness to redesign Tokyo. After the Great Kanto Earthquake, Prime Minister Gonbei Yamamoto appointed him as home minster to oversee the capital's reconstruction. The Imperial Capital Reconstruction Council and the Bureau for Reconstruction of the Imperial Capital were established, and Goto was named the bureau's chief.

Goto seized the opportunity as a perfect chance to rebuild Tokyo and quickly helped to map out a capital reconstruction plan. The plan included purchasing scorched land lots through public bond issuance and building a Western-style capital city by carrying out large-scale road improvement and land readjustment. The initial plan required spending as much as 3 billion yen, or twice the size of the national budget at the time.

His ambitious plan, dubbed "Goto's tall tale," was hampered by political strife, its budget was cut to several hundred million yen, and the Bureau for Reconstruction of the Imperial Capital was disbanded. The Yamamoto Cabinet resigned en masse in 1923 to take the blame for an assassination attempt on Crown Prince Hirohito (later Emperor Showa) by a communist agitator at the Toranomon intersection in Tokyo, and Goto resigned as home minister.

The Home Ministry's reconstruction bureau and the City of Tokyo succeeded the Bureau for Reconstruction of the Imperial Capital in implementing the reconstruction project. The Tokaido Line was fully restored within 1923 and the Tsukiji Fish Market also opened. In 1924, the Tokyo City bus service began, the Fraternity Memorial Hospital Foundation was established and construction of reinforced concrete Dojunkai apartment houses began. Streetcar operation was restored in the Ginza area, Eitaibashi Bridge over the Sumida River was completed, the Yokohama pier was repaired and Yamashita Park was built by reclaiming a former waterfront with rubble.

Construction of boulevards with disaster prevention capabilities began ahead of motorization, and water and sewage services, city gas and other infrastructure projects got underway. Goto's reconstruction scheme did not materialize as he had initially envisioned, but it laid the foundation for transforming Tokyo, crowded with wooden structures since the Edo feudal period (1603-1867), into a modern metropolis.

A ceremony to celebrate the completion of capital restoration enterprises was held in front of the Imperial Palace's Nijubashi Bridge in March 1930. Goto had died a year earlier.

エピローグ：東京今昔～100年を経て

Epilogue : Tokyo Past and Present over 100 Years

88. 焼け野原となった深川
Burned-down Fukagawa

焼け野原となった深川福住町付近（現在の江東区永代）。中央右の建物は第一国立銀行深川支店。その左と上方の大きな建物は渋沢倉庫。深川区は現在の江東区の西部に当たり、区内の8割以上が焼失した。東京大空襲でも区内のほぼ全域が焼失し、多くの死者が出る被害を受けた＝1923（大正12）年

A neighborhood of fire-ravaged Fukuzumi town in Fukagawa Ward (present-day Eitai, Koto Ward). On the center right is the Fukagawa branch of First National Bank. The big buildings on the left and above are Shibusawa warehouses. More than 80% of Fukagawa Ward (present-day western Koto Ward) was destroyed by fire. The ward, virtually obliterated, suffered many casualties in U.S. air raids during World War II. (1923)

89. かつての第一国立銀行深川支店跡
Ex-site of First National Bank's Fukagawa branch

江東区永代のかつて第一国立銀行深川支店があった交差点。土曜日の朝、広い永代通りを行く自転車＝2023（令和5）年5月27日

A crossing in Eitai, Koto Ward, where the Fukagawa branch of First National Bank once stood. (May 27, 2023)

90. 焼け落ちた吾妻橋の市電専用橋
Streetcar bridge burns down

焼け落ちた吾妻橋の市電専用橋（手前側）と人道橋。本所区（現在の墨田区）から浅草側を望む。右後方には浅草寺の五重塔などが見える＝1923（大正12）年9月

Azumabashi Bridge's burned-down streetcar bridge (foreground) and pedestrian bridge, as seen from Honjo Ward (present-day Sumida Ward) toward Asakusa. On the rear right is Sensoji Temple's five-story pagoda. (September 1923)

91. スカイツリー望む吾妻橋
Viewing Tokyo Skytree from Azumabashi Bridge

浅草寺に近く、橋のたもとには水上バス乗り場もあり観光客に人気のスポット。手前は台東区、向こう側は墨田区＝2023(令和5)年4月19日

Azumabashi Bridge today with Taito Ward (foreground) and Sumida Ward (on the other side). Sensoji Temple is nearby and a water bus stop is at the foot of the bridge, making the area a very popular tourist spot. (April 19, 2023)

92. 宮城前の天幕村

Tent village in front of Imperial Palace

楠《くすの》木《き》正成《まさしげ》の銅像を望む宮城外苑(現皇居外苑)にずらりと並ぶ避難者が暮らすテント(天幕)。大幕村と呼ばれたが、震災翌年の1月で村は解散した—1923(人正12)年

Tents for refugees fill the Imperial Palace Plaza (present-day Imperial Palace Outer Gardens) under the shadow of the bronze statue of samurai warrior Kusunoki Masashige. The tent village was dismantled in January. (1923)

93. 皇居外苑
Imperial Palace Plaza

楠木正成の銅像がある皇居外苑。東京駅に近く、緑が多い都心の貴重な空間。外国人観光客も多い＝2023（令和5）年4月21日

The bronze statue of samurai warrior Kusunoki Masashige is located in the Imperial Palace Plaza, which is close to Tokyo Station and attracts many foreign tourists. (April 21, 2023)

94. 銀座4丁目の惨状
Ginza 4-chome devastation

架線が垂れ下がり、焼けた自動車や市電が残る銀座4丁目交差点付近の惨状。中央奥は京橋方向で、当時高層ビルだった第一相互館が見える＝1923（大正12）年9月

Overhead wires of streetcars dangle and debris of cars and streetcars fill streets around Ginza 4-chome. In the rear center is the Kyobashi district where stood Dai-ichi Sogo Building, a high-rise structure at the time. (September 1923)

95. 銀座の歩行者天国
Pedestrian paradise

中央区銀座4丁目交差点。歩行者天国を歩く外国人観光客も多い＝2023（令和5）年4月30日

A car-free pedestrian zone near Ginza 4-chome crossing, attracting many foreign tourists. (April 30, 2023)

96. 壊滅的被害を受けた横浜桟橋
Yokohama pier suffers catastrophic damage

港湾施設が壊滅的被害を受けた横浜桟橋付近。復旧工事は震災直後から始まり2年後に竣工した＝1923(大正12)年9月

Catastrophic damage to port facilities around Yokohama pier. Restoration work began soon after the quake and was completed two years later. (September 1923)

97. 横浜港に客船
Cruise ships at Yokohama port

山下公園から見る横浜港大さん橋に接岸する大型客船「にっぽん丸」。山下公園は関東大震災のがれきを使い臨海公園として整備された＝2023（令和5）年4月28日

Luxury cruise ship Nippon Maru at Yokohama port, as seen from Yamashita Park. The park was built by reclaiming a former waterfront area with rubble after the quake. (April 28, 2023)

98. 被服廠跡の遺骨の山
A mountain of remains

本所の陸軍被服廠跡（現在の墨田区横網）に積まれた犠牲者のお骨と骨灰の山。被服廠跡で焼死した3万8000人の遺体はここで火葬された＝1923（大正12）年9月

A mountain of remains and ashes at the former Imperial Army Clothing Depot in Honjo (presently Yokoami, Sumida Ward). About 38,000 people perished and were cremated in the depot. (September 1923)

99. 東京都慰霊堂
Tokyo Memorial Hall

関東大震災で亡くなった人たちの遺骨を納めるため、震災で最も被害が大きかった被服廠跡に建立された東京都慰霊堂。1945(昭和20)年3月の東京大空襲などによる犠牲者の遺骨も納められている＝2023(令和5)年4月19日、東京都墨田区

Tokyo Metropolitan Memorial Hall in the former Imperial Army Clothing Depot. It was originally built for Great Kanto Earthquake victims but later added the ashes of victims of U.S. air raids during World War II. (Sumida Ward, Tokyo, April 19, 2023)

東京を支え続ける関東大震災──復興小公園と井下 清

武村　雅之
名古屋大学減災連携研究センター（地震学）

1. 帝都復興事業

大正12（1923）年9月1日に発生した関東大震災は平成23（2011）年の東日本大震災と比較すると、死者・行方不明者数は10万5000人で約5倍、人口比で約10倍。経済被害（直接被害）についてみても、被害総額は当時のお金で約55億円、GDP（またはGNP）比でなんと36.7%にもなり、これも東日本大震災（3.4%）の約10倍である。そのうち、東京市の被害は7割弱を占める。その根本原因は、道路や公園などの基盤整備を後回しにし、人口集中による木造密集地形成を放置した明治以来の都市政策の誤りにあった。

その反省にたって、震災後行われたのが帝都復興事業である。後藤新平や永田秀次郎（関東大震災当時の東京市長）さらには佐野利器《さのとしかた》（耐震構造建築の第一人者で帝都復興院理事兼建築局長）らが、必死に市民を説得し、「復興に勝る供養なし」の合い言葉の下に、合意形成が図られ、耐震・耐火を大前提として公共性を重視し、ロンドンやパリにも負けない首都としてふさわしい品格を備えた街づくりに東京は着手したのである。

その際の遺産は都心部のほとんどの道路や半数にも及ぶ橋梁など、今でも都民の生活を支え続けている。このほかにも、大半の地下鉄は、その際将来の建設を見越して幅員27㍍が確保された道路の下を走っている。

3大震災の比較

項目		関東	阪神・淡路	東日本
発生年		大正12年	平成7年	平成23年
地震規模M		7.9（8.1）	7.3	9.0
死者不明（人）		約10万5000	約5500	約1万8000
家屋被災世帯		約70万	約25万	約30万
経済被害	損害総額	55億円	9兆6000億円	16兆9000億円
	GDP	150億円	510兆円	490兆円
	GDP比	36.7%	1.9%	3.4%
	国家予算	15億円	71兆円	92兆円
	予算比	366.7%	13.5%	18.4%

関東大震災時はGDP（国内総生産）でなくGNP（国民総生産）
死者数には関連死は含まれていない

武村雅之（2018）『関東大震災がつくった東京』（中公選書）より

2. 復興小公園

そのような中で、人知れず子ども達や地域の人々を支え続けている施設がある。東京市がつくった52の復興小公園と旧来の5公園を移設改築した復旧小公園である。復興（旧）小公園は当時の小学校の敷地の狭さ解消のため、いずれも小学校に隣接して造られ、児童生徒が利用しない時は、一般市民が自由に散策できる場所として、また非常時には防火用地ともなり、避難場所ともすることが考えられたものである。

公園は子どもの運動を考えて6、7割は広場で、学校とは簡単に行き来できるようにし、広場のまわりに、あずまやや藤棚を設けて休憩所としたり、園内には子どもの遊戯場を設けて最新式の遊具をそろえたりした。また意匠には、瀟洒《しょうしゃ》な門や壁泉、露床、パーゴラなど西洋的なものを取り入れて飲用水栓やトイレも完備した。このため市民は家庭の延長として夕涼みなどに利用したり、集会・催物・ラジオ体操に利用したり、当時としては抜群に清潔な公衆トイレは毎朝人々の列ができるほどであった。市民にとって小公園は身近な世界にモダンな夢のような空間を与える地域のシンボルとなった。

3. 井下 清

「公園の父」と呼ばれた本多静六《ほんだせいろく》（林学者、造園家）が、隅田公園とともに世界に誇れると賞賛した復興小公園の生みの親は、当時、東京市役所の公園課の職員であった井下清《いのしたきよし》である。井下は、再開発が予定されていた両国の陸軍被服廠跡の一部が公園予定地であったことから、図らずも震災で最大の被害を出した同地で遺体4万体以上を荼毘《だび》に付す責任者となった。さらに横網町公園の整備、震災記念堂や復興記念館の建設にも奔走した。ところが試練はこれで終わらなかった。その後、第二次世界大戦の空襲で亡くなられた人々の遺体8万体を30カ所の都立公園に仮埋葬し、後日遺族に引き渡すという作業の陣頭指揮も執った。定年後すぐに東京都慰霊協会常務理事に就任、さらに1967（昭和42）年に理事長となった。まさに「人間の尊厳」を護るための一生であったといえる。

井下は震災前、わが国最初の公園墓地である多磨墓地(現在の多磨霊園)を完成させていた。他の自治体では人間の死体を不衛生物としてふつう衛生部局が葬送関連行政を行うが、井下には「生命の重さ・人間の尊厳」への深い思いがあった。今の東京都でも引き続き公園部局が葬送関連行政を担っているのは井下の思想に立脚してのことである。そんな井下が手掛けた復興小公園には、子ども達や地域の人々への深い愛情が込められていた。

復興小公園はほとんどが健在で、100年近くもその役割を果たし続けている。ただ残念なことに内部の設備は第二次世界大戦中の金属供出や空襲による被害などで多くが失われ、戦後も元どおりの姿に復旧されたものはない。唯一文京区本郷1丁目の元町公園は昭和57年の改修時に往時の姿に一応復元されたが、その後の管理が不十分で往時の姿を偲ぶにはほど遠い。

4. 東京の現在と未来を考える

第二次世界大戦の空襲で再び大きな被害を受けた東京は1964(昭和39)年の東京五輪への便乗に代表されるように、戦後、経済優先で効率化を進めるという名目の下、帝都復興事業の遺産を食いつぶしてきた。隅田公園の上に高速道路を通し、昭和通りの中央にあったグリーンベルトをつぶして立体交差の道路にし、水辺を破壊して明治の名橋日本橋や復興事業の大作である江戸橋を、事もあろうに高速道路の高架下に押し込めてしまった。

さらに最近、帝都復興事業のおかげで地震危険度が低いとされてきた都心部でも新たな問題が発生している。容積率緩和による超高層ビルの林立である。これによって、平時の過酷な通勤に加え、地震時の帰宅困難者問題やエレベーターの閉じ込め問題などが一層深刻になった。さらに今回の東京五輪で、洋上埋め立て地に大量に建設されたタワーマンションは、地盤の液状化などによって、地震時には「高層難民」を抱えて孤立する恐れもある。

街は市民の暮らしやすさを第一に考えなければならない。市民が住みやすい街にこそ防災も実現するのである。関東大震災から100年を機に、首都東京は市民が誇りに思えるような街を目指して、今こそ帝都復興事業に学ぶべきである。この写真展が、「関東大震災」という歴史を知り、今後の教訓として心に刻むきっかけになることを願ってやまない。

参考文献:武村(2023)『関東大震災がつくった東京ー首都直下地震へどう備えるか』中公選書

武村雅之(たけむら・まさゆき)
1952年、京都市生まれ。東北大理学部卒、同大大学院で理学博士修了。鹿島建設小堀研究室などを経て、2012年に名古屋大減災連携研究センター教授、20年から特任教授。この間、歴史地震研究会会長、中央防災会議専門委員なども務める。地震学の第一人者で17年には文部科学大臣賞(科学技術部門)を受賞。『関東大震災を歩く:現代に生きる災害の記憶』(吉川弘文館、2012)、『未曾有の大災害と地震学:関東大震災』(古今書院、2009)、『地震と防災』(中公新書、2008)ほか著書多数。

関東大震災から100年　これからの防災を考える

国崎　信江

危機管理教育研究所 代表／危機管理アドバイザー

私と地震防災のはじまり

横浜市で生まれ育った私は、関東大震災は80年したらまた起きる（当時は80年周期で起きると信じられていたようです）という周りの大人の声を耳にしながら育ちました。小学校でも関東大震災を学び、その不安から地震が来ないことを祈りながら寝ていました。

この影響なのか、私は危機管理アドバイザーとして活動をしています。きっかけは阪神大震災で、神戸は街並みが似ていたこともあり、関東大震災と阪神大震災の被害を重ね、直接的な被害はないもののわが事として衝撃を受け、以来地震から命を守る方法を探る道を今日に至るまで必死に歩んできました。

文明の発展と進化しない防災

当時横浜は、国内最大の貿易港として栄えており、外国人居留地には外国商館、銀行、ホテルなどれんがや石造りの洒落《しゃれ》た洋館が建ち並び、南京町（現：中華街）を含めて異国情緒あふれる商業都市として発展していました。このときの横浜はすでに44万人以上が暮らす大都市で、開港から近代都市へと60年をかけて発展してきました。

あれから100年。日本は近代都市化が進み、都市機能の集中化、人口増加、工業の発展により海岸の埋め立て造成、建物の高層化、地下空間の高度利用化が進められてきました。東京、名古屋、大阪に代表される大都市は、たいてい軟弱という地盤工学上の問題を抱えていて、大規模な災害が起きれば、揺れの増幅、液状化現象、地盤沈下、津波の浸水、大雨時には内水氾濫や地下空間への浸水などの高いリスクが潜在しています。

地球物理学者の寺田寅彦氏は、随筆「天災と国防」で「文明が進めば進むほど天然の暴威による災害がその劇烈の度を増すという事実である」という名言を残しています。私はいつも、多発する近年の災害被害の実態と訓練や防災学習の内容が見合っていないと感じており、文明の発展とともに災害の様相も変わり、災害で発生した事実こそがその時代を反映する教訓であるはずなのに、防災は昔のままで追いついていないと思っています。

主体的に行動する防災への転換

わが国には、地震調査研究推進本部、国家プロジェクトの戦略的イノベーション創造プログラム（SIP）、国立研究開発法人防災科学技術研究所等があり、日々の調査観測や研究開発による最先端の防災科学技術の成果が蓄積され実社会に利活用されています。しかし、国民の防災力向上に資するところまでは十分に反映されていません

たとえば、関東や東海地域の子どもたちが訓練で着用している防災頭巾は、綿やウレタン樹脂素材が多く、それが地震時の飛来落下物の衝撃にどこまで耐えうるのか、公的機関による科学的検証がなされないまま戦時中の防空頭巾の名残として使われ続けています。また、「揺れたら机の下」の指導は固定していない机に潜らせることが什器《じゅうき》の挙動を踏まえた科学的知見からも有効なのか、火災時に「濡れたタオルやハンカチで鼻や口をおさえる」指導は、一酸化炭素などの有毒成分を含む煙を吸って亡くなる人が多い実態を踏まえた指導であるのかなど、その時代に合った検証と指導が求められます。

先人の思想や知見を重んじつつも、昔と同じような事象が起きたとき、今の状況からどのような被害になり、どのような解決方法があるのかを防災の概念に縛られることなく、ましてや感覚的かつ不安定な要素のまま受け入れるのではなく、国や公的機関の科学的知見に裏付けられた根拠をもってその答えを一人一人が主体的に探り続けていくことが重要だと思っています。

新聞に期待するもの

巨大都市として施設や設備も近代化し情報伝達の手段も整備されると、人は、自らの力で災害の危険性を意識しなくとも、施設・設備を頼り、緊急時の速報や誘導に従って行動すればよい、という依存意識が強くなりま

す。とくに近年は計画書やマニュアルに重きがおかれ、自主判断の機会が失われているので、訓練で経験していないこと、マニュアルで想定していないことには思考停止状態になり、個人も組織も対応能力が弱まっているように思います。

関東大震災では流言飛語に惑わされ暴動や虐殺が行われました。通信手段が多様になった現代でも大規模な災害時にはデマが出ます。情報過多の社会では、自らがその情報の発信元、鮮度、広がりの範囲、自分が広めることの影響を見極める力をつける必要があります。その意味では、いつの時代でも被災者の拠り所になるのは新聞です。テレビやネットの情報はあっという間に流れて更新も早くじっくりと掴むことが難しいのですが、新聞は自分のペースで落ち着いて読めて、記録として保存することも容易です。また、回覧して情報を共有することで人々の動揺を抑える効果もあります。なにより新聞は報道だけでなく読む人に希望や未来を伝える力もあります。

今後新聞には、命を守る真の防災に向き合った、科学的知見からの防災情報の発信と、災害が起きたときだけではなく常に防災の情報に触れる機会を創出し、自らの命は自らで守れる力を育み、幾度となく襲う災害にしなやかに強く生き残れるように、日本の未来の安全安心に貢献する情報を発信し続けてくれることを期待します。

国崎信江（くにざき・のぶえ）
横浜市生まれ。女性や母親の視点による防災を研究し、2008年一般社団法人危機管理教育研究所を設立。20年以上にわたり第一線で防災・防犯・事故防止対策を提唱する。危機管理アドバイザーとして行政、企業、マンションなどのリスクマネジメントコンサルティングに携わるほか、省庁の検討・審査委員や自治体の防災アドバイザーなどを歴任。NHK総合ラジオ「マイあさラジオ」では「くらしの危機管理」コーナーに出演中。防災・防犯に関する著書多数。

色あせた百年前の鶴

カン・ハンナ
歌人／国際社会学者／タレント

私は韓国ソウル市生まれで、2011年、東日本大震災の2週間前に日本に来て以来、12年間日本で暮らしているニューカマーの韓国人です。そして1400年以上の歴史を持つ日本の伝統文学である短歌を通じて、日本での日々を私ならではの目線で伝えています。

カンさんは在日ですか?違います、ニューカマー、いえ異邦人です

チマチョゴリ、朝鮮学校、パッチギもニッポンに来て目にした歴史

殴り合うだけの世界に差別などないと在日のボクサーは言う

古き良き日本の文化が好きで自分の生活拠点を日本に移した私は、日本での暮らしをきっかけにいろいろ見えてくることがありました。良いことも悪いことも見逃せない立場になっているのでしょうか。隣国であるからこそ何百年以上の歴史のなかで複雑な関係性を持つのは当然なことかもしれません。とはいえ、韓国に住んでいた頃は自分とは直接関係のない遠い話に聞こえていたことが、今は他人事ではないと感じます。それは決して悪いことではないと思うのです。

先日、動画配信サービス「Apple TV+」で在日コリアンの世代を超えたストーリーがアメリカをはじめ海外で人気を集めているという話を聞いて興味を持ち、『Pachinko パチンコ』というドラマを見始めました。4世代にわたる在日コリアン一家の苦難の歴史を描いた作品でしたが、私はその作品の中で、1923年9月の関東大震災での朝鮮人虐殺事件を目の当たりにしました。関東大震災の混乱の中で「朝鮮人や共産主義者が井戸に毒を入れた」というデマが流れ、それを信じた憲兵隊や自警団などが多数の朝鮮人や共産主義者を虐殺した事件自体は耳新しい話ではなかったのですが、映像を通じて見聞きすると、より複雑な気持ちになりました。

正直なところ、この事件について私が100年前の当事者たちの気持ちを深く理解することはできないと思います。この事件に詳しくもない私が何かしらを発言すること自体がそもそも失礼に当たるのではないかと心配になります。しかし、一つだけ言わせていただけるならば、「過去と現在、そして現在と未来は私たちが思っている以上に繋がっていることを忘れてはいけない」ということです。

過去の痛みを覚えている人たちがこの世を去ったとしても、その子孫は今も生きています。そして、100年前の大きな地震が二度と起きないという確信はありません。もしこの先、大きな自然災害が起きた場合、過去が過去としてキレイに片付き、関東大震災での朝鮮人虐殺のような出来事は再び起きないと、私たちは自信を持って言えるのでしょうか。

ゆがんだ事実が一人歩きし、負の感情をあおることは、今の時代にも起きていることです。特に、SNSの発達により、情報の拡散力は100年前より大きい。しかも日本だけではなく、世界中どこの国でも起きているのです。気が付けば自分自身が被害者になる可能性もありますし、むしろ加害者になってしまう可能性もゼロとはいえません。特に大きな災害になるほど、多くの人が生命財産への不安を強く持ち、必死に情報を求めるようになり、その結果デマを信じてしまうことは、仕方がないことかもしれません。しかし、そのデマの対象になりやすいの

は、社会的マイノリティーです。とても残念ですが、どこかに隠れていた差別意識が表面化することになってしまうのです。

自然災害を未然に防ぐことはなかなかできません。ただ、過去の災害時に人々が起こした行動、事件を振り返り、過ちを未然に防ぐことはできるのではないでしょうか。決して日本だけの話ではなく、世界どこの国の人々にも大事な話です。また、今を生きている私たちの責任だとも思います。平和と平等を最も大事にする世界をつくれるのは、今の私たちなのです。

ミサイルや殺人事件が一面となる新聞で折ろうよ鶴を

そよそよと風が吹くようソウルでもサルランサルラン風は吹くだろう

カン・ハンナ(Kang Han-na)
韓国ソウル市生まれ。韓国でニュースキャスターやコラムニストとして活動後、2011年に来日。2019年12月に自身初の歌集『まだまだです』(KADOKAWA)を発表し、日本で歌人デビュー。同歌集で第21回現代短歌新人賞を受賞。現在「NHK短歌」(Eテレ)にレギュラー出演するほか、「未来世紀ジパング」(テレビ東京)、「堀潤モーニングFLAG」(TOKYO MX)などにも出演。横浜国立大学大学院都市イノベーション学府で博士号(社会学)を取得し、国際社会学者としても活動の幅を広げている。

関東大震災100年
—写真に刻まれた記憶—
定点観測者としての通信社

写真展

2023年8月18日(金)〜9月4日(月)
汐留シオサイト地下歩道 特設スペース

主催
公益財団法人新聞通信調査会

協力
共同通信社

総合企画
河原仁志(公益財団法人新聞通信調査会)

写真選定
君波昭治、飯岡志郎(共同通信社)

写真集

発行日
2023年8月10日

編集
公益財団法人新聞通信調査会
共同通信社

執筆
武村雅之(名古屋大学特任教授)
国崎信江(危機管理アドバイザー)
カン・ハンナ(歌人)
飯岡志郎(共同通信社)*コラム
君波昭治(共同通信社)*写真説明

和文英訳
米山司郎、菊田正憲、アントニー・ヘッド

制作
erA

印刷
中央精版印刷株式会社

発行人
西沢 豊

発行所
公益財団法人新聞通信調査会
〒100-0011 東京都千代田区内幸町2-2-1 日本プレスセンタービル1階
電話 03-3593-1081 https://www.chosakai.gr.jp

※大震災当時の写真取材事情に関するリポート「関東大震災100年」を共同通信社友・沼田清氏が月刊誌『メディア展望』に連載中です。当財団ホームページでお読みいただけます。

本書のコピー、スキャン、デジタル化等無断転載は、著作権法上の例外を除き禁じられています。本書を代行業者等の第三者に依頼してスキャンやデジタル化することは、個人や家庭内の利用であっても著作権法違反となり、一切認められておりません。

ISBN978-4-907087-21-0
©2023 公益財団法人新聞通信調査会/共同通信社

100 Years Since Great Kanto Earthquake
— Memories Captured in Photos —
A news agency as eyewitness

Exhibition

August 18 – September 4, 2023
Shiodome Siosite Underground Walkway Special Space

Organized by
Japan Press Research Institute

In cooperation with
Kyodo News

Executive Producer
Hitoshi Kawahara (Japan Press Research Institute)

Photo Selection Board
Shoji Kiminami, Shiro Iioka (Kyodo News)

Catalogue

Published on
August 10, 2023

Edited by
Japan Press Research Institute
Kyodo News

Contributors
Masayuki Takemura (Designated Professor at the University of Nagoya)
Nobue Kunizaki (Crisis Management Advisor)
Kang Han-na (Poet)

Authors
Shiro Iioka (Kyodo News) column
Shoji Kiminami (Kyodo News) Captions

Translated and edited by
Shiro Yoneyama, Masanori Kikuta, Anthony Head

Produced by
erA

Printed by
Chuo Seihan Printing corporation

Publisher
Yutaka Nishizawa

Published by
Japan Press Research Institute

The Japan Press Research Institute, in its monthly “Media Tembo” (Media Outlook), is publishing a series of articles on photo journalism at the time of the Great Kanto Earthquake 100 years ago, authored by former Kyodo News photographer and editor Kiyoshi Numata. You can read them on the institute's website.

All rights reserved. No part of the contents of this volume may be reproduced in any form whatsoever without the written permission of the publisher.

Copyright © 2023 by Japan Press Research Institute, Kyodo News